Behavioral Programming

Kelly Alwood

Alwood Tactical Innovations

Alwoodlocksport@gmail.com

www.behavioralprogramming.net

Printed in the United States of America

FOREWORD

Everyone eats every day, multiple times a day for many years, but just because everyone eats doesn't mean that everyone has a good grip on nutrition. You see that many people struggle with multiple eating patterns and many food options in the form of all these fad diets. In the same way, everyone talks and interacts with people every day but many of us struggle with this interaction in the form of miscommunication, angry tone, frustration, etc.

In order to achieve an optimal weight and body image, you need to change how your meal ingredients are chosen and cooked and you need a change in your lifestyle. You also need to make a change in how you think about yourself and how you think about others in terms of behavior and interactions in order to illicit an optimal relationship.

Kelly Alwood does an exceptional job in giving you the tools that you need to be able to elicit these changes. Down to the exact words needed and how to present them.

As the name of this book is Behavioral Programming, you need to understand that an interaction is a two-way street and you need to change your behavior and your mental programming to have a positive effect on the behavior of the person you are interacting with because the final outcome that everyone wants is a positive and healthy relationship.

In this book you will read about universal human characteristics in terms of behavior and communication, and you will learn how to identify a person's personality and what he values in a quick and effective way. What separates this book from many other books is the genuine message behind it, it's not about deception or manipulation, it's not a book about how can you detect if someone is lying to you. Many books start with the notion and precondition that there is an underlying battle and that a random stranger, or your loving spouse, is trying to lie to you and that's not healthy, even if these things are common. Reading with the intent of looking for these signals will install it in your subconscious mind and eventually you'll find them, or at least you will interpret every signal in a negative way without looking at the whole picture.

Instead, Behavioral Programming gives a healthy mentality and healthy ways that will help you to project your desires, and interpret other people desires, in a positive way that would eventually create the correct communication.

We are faced with multiple scenarios in our daily life, but the problem with many of the teachings regarding communication has to do with the generalized message. It will teach you about how to analyze a person and then how to communicate with him or "manipulate" him while missing the fact that it's all about context. Dealing with your spouse is totally different than dealing with your best friend. Dealing with your boss is totally different that dealing with your co- worker. Dealing with your friend is totally different than dealing with the clerk in the post office. These are all contexts that requires different measures mentally and emotionally from your side. This book will help you navigate these different scenarios in a comprehensive, yet easily understandable way.

The best way to communicate is face to face and everyone knows that, but many people prefer to text rather than talk on the phone. Texting gives you the advantage of communicating instantly without the need to wait for a perfect time or a perfect place, it gives you the time to respond without being on the spot, it gives you the time to check your facts and organize your thoughts. The problem with texting is that you can't fully project your emotions and your message can be received in a negative way. In the Digital Downloading chapter you will be able to see the common mistakes people make while texting. You will also learn how to communicate and how to influence using the convenience and the speed of modern technology.

I urge you to read this book with an open mind and take what you learn and apply it in your daily life. Absorb these universal principles and use every tool with the two pillars in mind. Test them and with time you will be able to write your own programming because no matter how individual we want to be, we are still part of a bigger group that can only thrive when we are honest in our communication.

Dr. Abdullah Alwardi

PREFACE

The human brain can be programmed like a computer. You just need to learn the code. Whether it's with a phone call, a text message, or face-to-face, you can train people very quickly to behave the way you want.

Can you make a stranger your friend in 5 minutes? Can you make your boss or coworker like you? Can you get a favor from a stranger? Can you get that loud, annoying person to respect you and see you as the Alpha? Can you change someone's mind? Can you convince someone to trust you in just a few minutes? Want more respect from someone? Want someone to stop harassing you?

This is a course on how to program people to do what you want them to do. In other words, how to generate the response from people that you desire. Whether it's getting a yes for a date or a sales pitch, soliciting help from someone, or stopping and starting a certain behavior, this book will teach you how to program the actions of other people.

The key to making friends is to give people what they want. We all want something. We all need something. We're all looking for something. Knowing what people want in a friend, and being what they want, is how you get results. You hear people say it all the time, "If I only knew what my wife wanted, I would do it," or, "If I knew what my friend needed I would give it to them," or, "If I knew what they wanted to hear at the interview, I would be prepared."

This book is about understanding people's wants and needs. Knowing what makes people happy, and doing it, is how to make people like you. When you truly make people happy, they want to be around you.

This book is about making friends and structuring long-term, productive relationships. From achieving a better working atmosphere with your boss and coworkers, to meeting and keeping a mate, to meeting and developing a relationship with a stranger, Behavioral Programming will teach you the techniques, key points, and information you need to influence people. You will learn how to start, build, and keep a real relationship.

This book will forever change the way you interact with people and the way people treat you!

Section 1: The Behavioral Programming System

This is how it all works and the rules you must follow to make it all set in successfully.

CHAPTER 1
HOW BEHAVIORAL PROGRAMMING WORKS

Making people feel good is one of the most basic instincts that all people have. It ranks up there with the desire for food. Everything you do is for one purpose. The most ornate and instinctive desire in humans is to feel good. There is nothing more organic than the good feeling a person gets. Every single thing you do in your life is in response to this desire to feel good. The reason you help other people is because it makes you feel good. The reason you go to work is because you get a good feeling about the results of your labors. The reason people use drugs, alcohol, and tobacco is all due to their most basic human desire to feel good and be happy.

Each of us, being individuals, doesn't desire the same things and the same things do not make us all feel good or happy. But what we do share is a common desire to feel happy. Everything you desire in your life is because you believe it will make you feel good. Love, money, sex, drugs, job, cars, house, pool, boat, whatever, everything in your life comes from the desire to feel good from it. Other systems try to manipulate people through their desires. However, many times these won't bring the results that you want because our individual desires differ, and when you do find a desire to fulfill it's often only one small piece of what someone really needs.

An example of this would be men using Neuro-Linguistic Programming (NLP) and other pick-up tricks to lure women into desiring them. This may work on some women, but the results are very temporary and false. The men will play to one or more desires in a woman to give her the sensation that she will feel good about certain actions. However, by the next morning the woman knows exactly what has happened.

Programming should only be done on relationships that need work, not established and matured relationships. This book will teach you how to achieve healthier relationships by programming others to behave in ways that will lead to greater happiness and a more fulfilling relationship for both of you. These techniques are not intended to be used with relationships that are not in need of modification. The techniques taught in Behavioral Programming are to be used to change behavior that does not help you both experience a healthy, productive relationship.

CHAPTER 2
THE TWO PILLARS FOR REAL SUCCESS

There are two components necessary for making Behavioral Programming work long term. These vital links to developing and building a real relationship are often overlooked. Rarely, if ever, does anyone address these two issues. Most information available is designed for short-term, non-authentic trust building (pick up artists, con men, interview success, etc.). Although those short-term techniques work for the purposes for which they were designed, they don't address the real components of a lasting friendship or relationship. They are based on trickery and deceit. The success that they seem to give is temporary. The principles laid out in this book will work as effectively for short term results, but have also been proven to work over the long term in establishing and maintaining productive relationships.

It's quite easy to trick people into liking you. However, the more a person gets to know you, the more evident it becomes that the person you first presented to them is not who you really are, or you have to work harder to keep up the impression that you initially portrayed to them. Making a relationship work long term is a different challenge.

The following two principles must be present from the beginning to make a real relationship work. As we discuss all of the different dos and don'ts throughout this book these two things will be our basis. These principles are critical to make Behavioral Programming work for the long term. Without these two principles, the techniques in this book would be for short-term use only. Pick up artists, con men and hacker social engineers will never discuss these two principles, as they never intend for their contact with others to achieve more than immediate self- gratification. Mutual Benefit and Honesty must be the base layer, the two pillars of success, that all other Behavioral Programming techniques are built upon in order to cultivate real, lasting relationships.

The First Pillar: Honesty

The first foundational element is honesty. It's impossible to have a real relationship without honesty. If you're not honest, then the person you have a relationship with doesn't really like you; they like the person you're pretending to be. Sooner or later, the truth will come out and they will find that they really don't like you, that this whole time they learned to enjoy the company of someone else, and you aren't that person.

Some people have things that they just can't tell to people who are close to them. Many occupations require secrecy. Undercover police, attorneys, doctors, military or intelligence agents, R&D workers, and many others all require an element of secrecy for their work. For this, the details of work should not and cannot be disclosed. In these types of cases, you simply don't disclose any information to anyone that they don't need to know. You don't lie about it, you simply tell people that are close to you that you can't discuss details of your work. Deep undercover, and "secret" operations may require more discretion than others, but that's a very small handful of us out in the day to day world. Leaving out details of things we're mandated not to disclose to others isn't lying, it's just part of real life.

Lying is telling an untruth. We can all avoid lying. Even when you're asked questions that you don't want to answer, you simply don't answer them. Do not lie about them. Change or redirect the subject, or simply state that you can't talk about that right now. In a real, long-term relationship, all of the lies will eventually come out. We'll discuss giving personal details in a later chapter, but for now we have a foundation of honesty. It is always better to avoid a subject or refuse to answer than it is to lie about it.

If we look at short-term relationships, we can always find a tipping point as to when it all started going south. Many times it is because one person caught the other in a lie. The actual act or deed that was lied about is most often forgiven, but the lie is what seals the deal of mistrust. You can never have a healthy friendship with someone who doesn't trust you. So when a friend discovers your lie, the trust is gone, taking away the true friendship. Your relationship with that person will never be the same again.

Everyone makes mistakes and everyone can forgive most actions. However, no one ever forgets when they catch you in a lie. Because the other person has most likely done some of the same things you've done, it's easy for them to forgive you. But if you lie to them, they do not forgive and forget the lie.

It's very easy to lie to someone that you just met. That person doesn't know you from Adam. However, as you spend time with them and you begin to get to know each other, the truth will start to come out quickly. The way most people deal with this is to just keep lying, compiling the mess. Pretty soon you can't keep your story straight, and you realize that the only reason this person has any interest in being with you is because they believe that you're someone else. In most cases this will end the relationship.

As we go through the details of making and keeping real friends in the following chapters keep in mind that everything must be done with honesty as your first pillar of success.

The Second Pillar: Mutual Benefit

The second pillar of relationships is Mutual Benefit. This is another component that most everyone leaves out of their behavioral programming instruction. Without the principle of Mutual Benefit you're only building a short- term, self-serving relationship that cannot and will not last.

Everyone has had that one so-called "friend" that used you, that one person that never benefited you, but was always a drag on your resources. They never gave back. You need to approach every relationship with an eye toward mutual benefit. Both sides have to benefit from the relationship or it won't last.

There are many ways to benefit from others. For some, simply helping a person is a benefit to them. It makes them feel good. For others, they may benefit from your advice and life experiences. Whatever it is, both people need to gain from the other. You can't have a healthy long-term relationship with a user. When you seek to add a friend to your ranks, you must have something genuine to offer them as well.

Another situation that often turns into a tipping point in a relationship is when one person is doing all of the work. When this happens, the other person is getting no benefit from it anymore.

Some people we really want in our lives, others are thrust upon us by work or other social mandates, however, having the ability to make these into comfortable working relationships is what makes life a lot easier.

****

I was sitting in Kuala Lumpur, Malaysia one humid afternoon. I was with a friend at an Indian restaurant, discussing a business meeting he was going to after lunch that afternoon. This man is a very successful businessman and probably the most ethical businessman that I have ever met. He started to explain to me how he would approach his upcoming business meeting. He would design this meeting the same way he plans them all, in such a way that everyone wins.

He explained that a long-term business relationship can't be made if only one side wins. He went on to tell me that all parties must win and benefit from the deal. If more than two parties are involved, then all must be happy and win. If one party does not feel benefited from the relationship, the whole will be affected.

I realized at that point that this was true for any relationship. All parties involved must benefit, or the relationship will not last. One side will be used, and the other will be the only winner. Now this isn't a selfish thing, and benefit takes many forms. But for anyone to want to stay involved with you, there must be some kind of added value. They need to add value to your life in some way. Just the same, you must add value to the other person's life to keep their friendship. If you approach each relationship with this in mind, you will be successful in keeping your relationships long term. When everyone wins, it just works out.

CHAPTER 3
THE FOUR CORNERSTONES OF BUILDING RAPPORT

These are the four keys to building rapport quickly with someone. Using one, or a combination of these will enable you to speedily get on the good side of someone in moments. Here are the four cornerstones:

1. Common Enemy
2. Siding Goals
3. Agreement
4. Random Favors

You will see these used throughout this book. Many different examples are presented of how to use these to program people for a different, more desirable behavior.

Here's how they work. The first technique is to find that of finding a Common Enemy. This is quite simple to do most of the time. It doesn't take long at all for you to talk to someone and find that one piece of information that you need to implement this technique. You see, everyone has many things in common. Most of the time people in society focus on our differences. By changing the angle at which you view people you can find things in common with them, things that make you relate to each other, things that will bring you closer and build a lasting friendship.

You can speak with a person very briefly and figure out who is a burden in their life. We all have them. We all have those people in our lives that make our lives more difficult and uncomfortable. Whether it be at work, home, or in society, we all have those people that we don't like. So as you talk to your new acquaintance, look for that person in their life that makes it difficult, and relate that same type of burden in your own life.

I will give you an example. You are talking to your phone carrier on the phone, trying to get a charge taken off your bill. By having a quick conversation with the person, not going straight to "shop talk," you will begin to get friendly with them. During this brief moment you mention their boss. This is usually a pretty safe target, because most people do not like their boss or feel they enrich their lives. You may make a simple statement such as; "I bet your boss doesn't realize how difficult your job is, dealing with upset people all day." They will likely say, "Yes, he doesn't have to deal with them all day, but he sure tells us what to do."

So now you must show them how this relates to you. Explain to them how they are not alone, and you have a boss just like that too. Show this person that you share a "common enemy." Tell them how your boss doesn't realize what "we" have to go through every day and how "we" need to stick together. "We need to help each other because our bosses don't care." This is something that person on the phone can relate to. You have now found a common enemy. When you now ask them to help you with that charge on your bill, you will find them feeling sympathy for you as you have just shared one another's pain, through a common enemy.

You can do this with anyone out there. No matter how different you are from the other person, you can find that one person or entity in your lives that makes you both miserable at times. Focus on this new angle when talking with people you don't know, and even people that you may not get along with very well. You will find the common enemy, and this will put you on friendly ground. You will see this technique used with other rules throughout this book. There are many ways to adapt and combine this technique to program people to behave in a way that builds your relationship.

The second strategy is Siding Goals, which is divided into two possible approaches. One way is quite polite and passive, the other way is direct and aggressive. They both work; you will get the action or behavior that you want out of that person in the end, but only one will build a good relationship and can be used again with that person. The other will burn the bridge and is therefore a one-time shot and not to be used in building long-term relationships.

Siding Goals works similarly to the Common Enemy approach, but works a different angle. In this technique you don't look for a common bad; rather, you demonstrate a common good. You will align their goals with yours. This can take many forms, and be used in innumerable circumstances. One example is the use of Siding Goals in negotiating a purchase. Let's say you are shopping for a car. This car is something that you need and want, and you will buy it if they will adjust the price a bit. At the current price they are offering, you will say no. You don't need it that badly.

What you do is to find a way to align their goals with yours. Bring them onto your side by helping them see that their goal is the same as yours. In this case, their goal is to make a sale. You can use that knowledge to align them with your goal of getting a good deal. Tell them that you would like to buy the car, but you can't spend that much money. Your desire to buy the car is perfectly aligned with their desire to sell the car. Now your goals and his goals are aligned. Now you are on the same team. Now he will work with you to adjust the price to make his sale (your purchase) feasible. His sale, and your purchase have become the same goal. You brought him onto your side.

When you arrived at the dealership, you were not on the same side. He was on the selling team to make money, and you were on the losing, spending money team. His job started out trying to convince you to buy a new car. When you align your goals, it will now benefit him to help you with what you need. This is the polite and passive way to align your goals with someone.

The aggressive and direct way to achieve Siding Goals is as follows, but its use should be limited to those situations where you have no desire for a long-term relationship with the other person. From a real life story, I'll show you how it works.

****

My friend Kevin and I were on a road trip. He and I stopped at an office supply store to print off student binders for a class the next day. We entered the store at about 6:30 PM. The store closed at eight pm. We went to the print station, gave them our thumb drive and asked them for 25 copies of the entire PPT. The store manager happened to be the one working at the print station. He plugged in the thumb drive and opened the file. He noticed that the file was quite large, and would take some time to print, especially to complete our request for 25 copies of it, bound and organized.

He handed us back the thumb drive and explained to us that he would not print them, as there was not enough time to get it all done before the store closed.

We were very disappointed. We had no other option. Class started in the morning and we needed it done now. This guy would not budge. He would not submit to any other form of behavioral programming that we tried. He just flat out refused. We had wasted another 30 minutes trying to convince him. It was now seven o'clock and we hadn't even started to get what we wanted. At this point several things were obvious. He had no desire to help us. He would not change his mind for our benefit. Additionally, his resistance told me the one piece of information that I needed. He had somewhere to be at eight o'clock. He was not willing to chance being late for our benefit.

This is where Aggressive Goal Siding came in. We would force him to be on our side. Our goal was getting our material printed and out the door by eight pm. Soon he would have the same goal. What happened when we looked at him and said, "I have no other option, I must get this done tonight. If I don't get what I want, then I will make sure you do not get what you want. I know you have to be out of here right at eight o'clock. I will not let that happen if I don't get what I need."

I told the man that I would remain in the store until 8 o'clock, and at that time I would refuse to leave. I would have a bunch of things in my hand that I would want to purchase, but wouldn't be able to find my credit card or all of the coupons that I would want to use in a timely manner. I would wait for him to call the police to have me removed from the store. Then I would explain to them that I lost my wallet in the store. I made sure that he knew that I intended to delay him as long as possible. If I couldn't get what I wanted, then he wouldn't get what he wanted. He realized that I was dead serious. At this point he realized that we had the same goal. His goal was now "be out of here by eight p.m. with material printed." After coming to the conclusion that this was the most likely outcome, he went right to work printing our material as needed, for we now had the same goal.

Agreement is the next way to get on someone's good side quickly. One thing that irritates us all is when you are talking to someone and they counter and argue about everything you say. Few people are more annoying than that guy. The opposite of that guy is the person who listens to what you are saying and agrees with you. What is even better is after they agree with you they add value to the conversation. This is what you need to do to build rapport. Listen to what the person is saying, and find a common interest and voice your agreement with them.

Of course we do not all agree on everything, but we don't have to. Listen to people and agree with a portion of what they say. You can always find some part to agree on. You should avoid disagreement, and focus your attention on finding what you can agree on from what they are saying. When you agree with people, they will connect with you and feel a bond. An example might be, you sit down to lunch with a new co-worker. They start a conversation with you about sports. You actually care nothing about sports and think professional athletes are overpaid knuckle draggers.

This would normally end the interest of building a relationship or rapport with that person. But let's keep going. You listen intently to what they are saying; you are trying to find something in what he says that you like as well. He is talking about professional sports, so you find you can agree with him that professional athletes are fit and fitness is also an interest of yours.

When you are truly listening to another person and looking for something to find in common and agree with, you will do just that. Most people spend their time not actually listening to what another is saying, but thinking about the first few seconds of what the other person has said and then their thoughts are on what they will say in reply. When the other person pauses they jump right in with their already rehearsed lines. This does not build rapport. This shows that you are not really listening and is the opposite of agreement. Think about this; every time you heard someone report to you about a person they just met and liked, they always say "we had so much in common, I really like him/her. We like the same music/color/shoes/pizza," or whatever it may be. This is critical to building rapport. On the same note, think of every time that you gave a report about meeting someone that you didn't like. You described your meeting as, "He was a liberal jerk," or, "She was a sleazy girl," or, "He actually thinks ....". All of these are statements of disagreement. You summed up your whole experience with that person in the fact that you did not agree. So now you know; find things you can agree on and focus on those things. You will build rapport in one conversation.

Random Favors is the last cornerstone of this discussion. Simply put, this is a way of doing a good deed for someone without them asking, so they owe you kindness in return. The most simple example of Random Favors is to hold the door open for someone. They did not ask you to do so, but they are grateful and now owe you a debt. No matter how small the debt may be, they now owe you. Even if you are paid with a smile, or a thank you, they owed you that and you got it without asking for it.

How do you get someone to smile at you or talk to you that otherwise wouldn't? You Random Favor them. Now they are obligated under social etiquette to show you kindness. The rules of society dictate that you cannot be cruel to someone who just did something nice for you.

Now let's take this to a different level. Let's go back to the car lot. You are looking to buy a new car again. Not only can you use the Siding Goals, tactic, you can also use Random Favors. How would the salesman react if you brought another buyer with you to the lot? You have just done him a favor, without him asking for it. You just did a Random Favor for him. By doing him this favor, bringing him another customer and the chance to make another sale, he now owes us an act of kindness. What you would naturally expect or accept as kindness in return is a good deal on your new car. You can now tell him that if he works with you to give you the price you need you will both be willing to buy a car from him that day. That adds a whole new level to the Siding Goals.

At every stage of the game you can always take it up a notch. You scale the approach to fit the demand. How much information you give out, how far you go to help another person all depends on what behavior or reaction you need to get from them. It's really like The Golden Rule. You will do something for someone that you want them to do for you. You will help them feel good about you, comfortable with you, and know that they can trust you. By knowing what people want, and what makes them comfortable you can make people happy very quickly. You can be a better friend when you know what the other person actually wants or needs in a friend.

Upon these four cornerstones, and our two pillars, you will build the foundation for great relationships. You must start with these, and always use them first. Once these are in place, you can follow the rules in the next chapters to build a strong, lasting, drama-free relationship with anyone you desire. The human brain is like a computer, and you can program it for the desired response if you know the code.

Kevin and I have spent many hours together over the years discussing and testing these methods all over the world. They are consistent. Learn the original source code for the human brain, and then you can reprogram it because you know how it works. What we do not want to do is simulate a course of actions and speeches that you memorize and spit out to people from memory. That tactic is used by many systems in many other books. The fact that thousands of people are using the same exact lines from those books on everyone they meet tells you that they are not sincere. The relationships that you develop on false pretenses will never be real. Those methods build a relationship on cookie-cutter lines and dishonesty.

The purpose of building rapport is to build a real, healthy relationship quickly with a person. Once you have that rapport (your foundation), you can then build the rest of the house. This is the way to quickly and efficiently get the ball rolling with someone you wish to befriend. Your goal for this is to leave people feeling better than before they met you. Follow these initial steps to build rapport with a person, and the chapters that follow will help you grow and maintain healthy, lasting relationships.

SECTION 2: HUMAN DEFAULT PROGRAMMING

Human Default Programming means the way your brain is programmed to function from birth. This is how you think and how your brain coding controls your behavior. You must understand the operating system and its code to know how to change the code.

CHAPTER 4
Organic Psychology

Behavioral Programming is organic psychology. It's an all natural, organic, and healthy way to enter and code a person's brain for specific behavior and responses. To use this approach you need to look at your relationships with others as a living ecosystem, constantly evolving and changing through your interactions. Because Behavioral Programming works off of the two pillars of honesty and mutual benefit, this makes the alterations that you are doing natural and easy. Organic psychology is using the natural stream of information flow to program a person for a healthy response.

Our lives are all intertwined with the lives of others. Look at your relationships with others as a living ecosystem. It can be fragile, complex, and requires effort to maintain. It's natural and alive, and things will naturally happen. Things can really start to go off track when you introduce foreign chemicals into the ecosystem. Chemicals will alter our ecosystem and the way it functions. Chemicals in our relationships are things such as deceit, greed, and all other unnatural or inorganic techniques and emotions that you might use on people in your attempts to manipulate their behavior.

On the other hand, things that are organic work in harmony with your system of relationships and things flow along smoothly. Many books have been written on how to manipulate and influence people by introducing "chemicals" into their relationship ecosystem. These are unnatural and unhealthy ways of forcing people to do what you want them to do. This is not only unnecessary, but is harmful to the natural cycle of relationships. Behavioral Programming works by coding the brain with natural and instinctive impulses and behavior. It works from the most primal needs so it is natural and healthy for them and for you.

Usually you will find that there is only one best way to accomplish a goal. Many other ways may exist, but only one will produce the most desirable outcome. Similarly, there are many ways to alter a person's behavior and responses, but the approach we advocate is natural, healthy and green. Using other methods to manipulate another's behavior is like dumping bleach and toxins into the river. It will have unforeseen, and unnatural repercussions to that person and to your relationship with them. Keep your relationships natural and healthy. You can get the results you want by going green.

Foreign "chemicals" will be unpredictable outside of very specific circumstances. Learn to code the brain naturally, and everyone involved will benefit.

CHAPTER 5
FOUR HUMAN CHARACTERISTICS

There are four characteristics commonly found in people. These four things should be kept in mind whenever you are trying to change a person's behavior. You can use these in conjunction with, or separately from, the four cornerstones of building rapport. Listed below are specific examples of each so you can see how they work and can be applied. Kevin Reeve noticed these four characteristics in his research and teaches these in his classes. Through the years we've tested and proven these characteristics with hundreds of our students. The four characteristics are:

1. People want to help those in need: Caretakers
2. People want to avoid unpleasantness: Peacemakers
3. People want things that are hard to get: Achievers
4. People respect authority figures: Constituents

1. People want to help those in need: Caretakers

We term those people with the strongest instinct to help others the

"Caretakers." This is something that must be put in the right context. Often in our society, people can seem to not want to help other people. People will, in some cases, watch as others are beaten, mugged, and worse in public while walking by and pretending not to see anything.

This is a basic instinct in most people. However, location and society dictate how well this one works. The larger the city, the more cold people tend to be. If a person has the most basic characteristics of a decent person, this one will work. When you do come across those callous individuals, you may have to use the aggressive method of Siding Goals to get them motivated to help you. Under normal behavior we all like to help people. It makes us feel good about ourselves. We all need this. In a way, service to others is a way of helping ourselves. We feel good when we help others and so that's our reward. We really don't need any other compensation for helping those in need. You can talk to anyone who volunteers time in their community or church, they'll tell you that they do it because it makes them feel better. They feel good about themselves. You can sometimes cheer someone up and improve their day by asking them for help. I have done this on many occasions. I have asked someone for help although I really didn't need the help. They needed to feel needed and wanted. They needed to feel good. Maybe they're just having a bad day, and helping you will make them feel better. This is completely in line with our two pillars approach. We'll get the help we need, and the other person will be compensated with emotional wellness.

How do we actually implement this behavior change? We must present ourselves to them with a need. We must express to them in some way that we're in need of help. This may be by direct statement "I need your help," or it may be perceived through your actions by the other person. The caveat to this is that we must also present the notion that they hold the solution to our problem. Most likely if it's something that they can do with little cost to themselves, they'll do it to help us. We have a much higher probability of success if we actually present ourselves for help. We need help. We can't do it ourselves. We don't present it as a favor to us. We present it as something we need, and we can't get it done without their help.

First, when we ask for help it makes the other person feel powerful. No matter how big or small the request, they realize that they're in a position of power with us because they can make this thing happen. Without them we can't make it happen.

Now that we have them feeling a bit powerful, we must demonstrate our need. Immediately tell them the reason that you need their help. You do this by explaining the consequences if you do not get help. At this point they're getting emotionally vested in helping us. They now must know what it is that you need and how they can help you get it. We then present the need in a minimized way. This doesn't mean we lie about the details or the extent of the help that is required, it means that we present what we need, focused on the basics and not making it sound like a major operation on their part. The last part of this is taking away their number one reason to say no. Let's face it, we've all been asked for help and we've not always helped out. There's a reason that you didn't help them.

The first thing that people do is try to immediately assess whether or not you truly need the help you've requested. Then they ask themselves if you deserve the help or whether or not you got yourself into the jam. We all do this. It's the first thing that goes through our heads. If we've decided that they do in fact need and warrant our help, then we try to discern how much this will cost us in time, energy, money, reputation, etc. If you make it to this point in your mind, you will most likely end up helping that person with what they need.

So now that we know the formula, let's make this easy for the person to help us. First we must present them with our need. The best way to do this is to let the person see it and not ask for it. At this point we haven't asked for it, they have volunteered it and we are golden. An example of this could be a flat tire. You're driving by and see a vehicle with a flat on the side of the road. You pull over to help. At this point you're already hooked. You wouldn't think about pulling over, getting out, asking them if they need help, they say yes and then you leave. No one would do that. You wouldn't have stopped in the first place. So by making it obvious through your actions that you need help, you actually have a much higher rate of success than actually asking for it. Let them ask you if you need help.

If we can't effectively demonstrate our need for help through actions, then we must ask. So remember the first thing they will assess is whether you really need it and deserve it. As soon as you get their attention, you need to tell them why you need the help. "I need $5 for fuel to get to the soup kitchen where I serve meals, I forgot my wallet at home."

That type of request will demonstrate the first two criteria. First, you are not doing this for your own benefit, so you deserve it for doing something good; someone else is benefited as well if they help you. Second, you demonstrate a true need for help as all of us have left without our wallet or purse at some point and can sympathize with your predicament. We immediately cured the "cost to them" concern by stating our request for only $5. How, at this point, can they say no?

People want to help others in need. Take away their doubts about you and your motives. Give them a feeling of doing good. Give them a sense of power. Make the cost affordable to them as to not be a big burden on them, or at least make it comfortable for them to burden themselves by helping you.

2. People want to avoid unpleasantness: Peacemakers

Many people instinctively want to avoid confrontation. We call these people Peacemakers. It is true for most people that they don't want to be the cause of discomfort or suffering in another. Knowing this gives us some real leverage when programming them to behave in a certain way. Let's look at an example.

****

During a class Kevin asked his students to infiltrate a convention. The class was mostly made up of DOD Security Contractors, all younger-to-middle-aged men. The convention that happened to be going on that day was a sorority reunion. It must have been from the class of 1910 because these women were very old. After several attempts the students could not talk their way into the convention. Kevin decided to show them how it was done. He walked into the lobby with a distressed look on his face and his phone in hand. He didn't say a word. He paced back and forth for a few minutes, looking anxious and frustrated. He put the phone to his ear and then back down. More pacing. At this point the lady behind the desk couldn't take it anymore. She asked, "Can I help you?" Kevin replied, "Yes, my wife was supposed to meet me out here in the lobby 30 minutes ago and she isn't answering her phone. Can I go in and find her, please?" The lady smiled and said, "Of course." The students looked on with astonishment as he walked into the convention hall.

Kevin used characteristic number two. As a rule, people don't like to see others uncomfortable. It's unpleasant to watch someone who is frustrated.

Knowing this, Kevin demonstrated his discomfort to the lady. She could feel his frustration. This appealed to rule number two; she didn't like watching Kevin's discomfort. She wanted do something about it. Then he applied the rules from characteristic one; she had a chance to help relieve his discomfort, and it cost her very little to do so.

3. People want things that are hard to get: Achievers

We call these people "Achievers." Things that are hard to get are automatically more desirable. The tactic here is to convince the person that what you have is something that most people don't. Let's say it would be mutually beneficial for you to program your friend to stop making jokes at your expense.

You can use this technique to program their behavior to do just that. In this scenario you would make yourself appear to be highly desired by others, or make yourself unavailable to them. In either case you are now hard to get, making you desirable to your friend. They will now realize your worth and change their behavior because once something is valuable and hard for us to get, we treat it with respect. It didn't come easy so we have to take care of it. We won't take it for granted.

You could make it a point to notify your friend that others are wanting your time and attention. "Joe called me again today, he really wants me to go hang out with him." Or, "Sara came by today to tell me about her new boyfriend and get some advice." Creating competition will automatically make something harder to get. You created competition for your friend, and now they'll have to work to be your friend. It's not a "gimme" anymore.

Do these hold up to our two pillars? Sure they do. We'll both benefit by our friend not joking about us. We will be closer and stronger. We were honest about another's desire for our attention and time. There is nothing wrong with demonstrating our real value. Sometimes people just forget how lucky they are to have you, or new acquaintances just don't know yet what a good person you are to have in their circle.

4. People respect authority figures: Constituents

The respect for those who appear to have authority over us is common in all societies. We call those people who strongly display this characteristic, "Constituents." Though the actual figure might be different, every culture and society has authority figures that they respect. A sure sign of an authority figure is a "scepter of authority." This is a trademark accessory that everyone can recognize. An example is a police badge, an orange vest and stop sign, a clipboard, a name tag, or even a uniform. All of these things represent some form of authority. Most of us in society don't have these things with us in our daily lives. Therefore, anyone who has one is seen as someone of authority.

A great example is a school crossing guard. They come in all shapes, sizes, and ages. They walk in front of moving traffic and raise their little stop sign and everyone stops. Did you ever stop to ask yourself what kind of authority or power they actually have? Probably not. Could the crossing guard arrest you and handcuff you if you didn't stop when they put up their sign? Could they impound your car? Give you a ticket? No, but when they step out and hold that sign up you stop. They are authority figures, though they have no real authority. The same goes for utility workers and road crews. They have no arrest powers. They can't chase you down. They can't even write you a ticket. But we all respect them and stop when the hold up the sign.

Knowing this, we can use this to program a response or behavior from someone. One way to get someone to change behavior is to possess power over them that will force them to change. An example is your boss. He has programmed you to behave a certain way with him. If you didn't, he would fire you. He has that authority. So what we need to do is to convince our target that we are in a position of authority. It doesn't even have to be directly over them.

First, being an authority figure automatically gives you status as an Alpha. Second, being an authority figure demands respect and certain etiquette towards you. This plays out all sorts of ways. Basically, if you act like you're in charge, or a boss, people will assume that you are. So, if you act like an authority figure, people will not challenge it. They'll normally just accept it. Confidence is a huge part of this. You must demonstrate confidence with others. Everyone has noticed how a police officer takes charge when he shows up and interacts with the public. No one is left to wonder who has the authority. Their confidence is high, and they are demanding.

We will discuss this further in other sections, and how this works with body language and how it can be used as a tool. Just keep in mind that people respect authority figures, and that you need to be seen by people as a person of authority. This doesn't mean that you need to lie about who you are, or what position you hold, it means that you must be seen as a leader, or someone with authority in the situation. You may be the most knowledgeable person on a certain topic. That makes you an authority figure to that person or group. You may be the strongest warrior of the group; that makes you the authority in that arena.

Find whatever it is that you do better than most others around you. Focus on those things to present yourself as an authority. Any past or present position or title can make you an authority figure. "I'm an Eagle Scout," or "I was the shooting team captain," or "I am a small business owner." Whatever it is that you've done, others around you don't have the same life experience or knowledge and expertise that you have in certain areas. That's one of your added values. To many people you are an expert in something.

These are four basic characteristics that will help you to program people to do what you need them to do. Knowing how they already think and how their brains are programmed will help you alter their behavior.

You will see how these four things are constantly in use while in conjunction with other points in this book. We'll use one or more of these four with other rules to program the behavior of others. These are always used with our two pillars, Honesty and Mutual Benefit, for success.

CHAPTER 6
AFECT

This is a test that can be done by anyone in almost any social environment. The Alwood Field Expedient Characteristic Test, the AFECT, will allow you to quickly evaluate someone to determine what type of characteristic trait drives them and their actions. This will help you to build rapport and make a connection with people very quickly and effectively.

The four human characteristics listed in this book are the most prevalent and easiest to build rapport with. However, they are different characteristic traits and all of them will not work with the same effect on everyone, as everyone is unique because of their unique genetics, environment and interactions with others.

This entire book is about specifics. It is about addressing specific behaviors with specific people. It is about personalized and intimate interaction. We do not focus on generalities. Rather, we view everyone for their own character and traits and respect them as individuals. With this in mind we will use this test to determine what is their most dominant characteristic trait so we know what is important to them in their lives, and we will try to connect with them through that characteristic trait.

To do this test all you need is a third party individual or group to be within view of the subject of the test. The third party should be one or more individuals that your test subject does not know. There should be at least one member of the third party group who is the same sex as your test subject. If your test subject is male then there needs to be at least one male in the third party group for you to accurately test your subject. The reason for using the same sex is so that your test subject can relate to, and ultimately identify with that person. This allows your subject to think they are talking about the stranger, when in reality they will describe themselves in that person.

What we are going to do is to innocently ask our test subject to look at another person, a stranger to them, and ask what they think is going on with that stranger and what they are thinking or talking about. For example, you are in a restaurant with your new friend, the subject of your test. You look over at a couple at another table and ask your friend (test subject), "What do you think is going on at that table; what are they talking about?"

What we want them to do is to tell us a story about what is going on, not just describe the scene. No matter how brief their "story" of the subjects and event, we can gather needed information. However, the more detailed they are in the story, the more information we can gather and the more accurate the results will be.

What we are looking for are the words that they use in their story such as "I" or "they" or "we" or "us" etcetera. The other thing we are listening for in their story or explanation of the subjects and events is the "why." Why are they doing what they are doing? This will give us a good base of information to work from to determine what characteristic trait is most important to them. This will tell us how to focus our conversations and interactions with them. The four traits that we are looking to identify in our test subject are the following:

- Caretaker
- Achiever
- Constituent
- Peacemaker

These personality traits are marked by the following motivations:

- "People want to help others in need" (Caretaker)
- "People want things that are hard to get" (Achiever)

31

- "People respect authority figures" (Constituent)
- "People want to avoid unpleasantness" (Peacemaker)

Once we determine what is a person's most dominant characteristic, we will use the relevant approach to build rapport with them.

The Caretaker can be identified by their answers or stories that focus on social things. A "social caring" motivated person, the Caretaker will be influenced by the social merits of the situation. Social interactions, feelings, relationships, but no conflict. These are all signs of a social caretaker, and this will put them into the first category of "people want to help others in need."

For instance, you are with your friend in the restaurant and you ask them what is going on with a couple at another table. The Caretaker will offer an explanation such as, "the woman wants to do something for her husband because he had a bad day, so she took him out to eat." Or, "that guy wants to cheer her up so he took her out to eat." Their story will involve emotional motivation, feelings, and relationships. They will often derive a story of someone helping someone else, revealing a kind thought behind the action. These people demonstrate a strong characteristic of wanting to help others. This would most likely be the most effective way to connect with that person, by using the techniques discussed in that chapter.

The second character type, the Achiever, will give you a different set of key words and stories. They will look at the exact same scenario and present you with a completely different story about what is going on. The second type of person is the achiever and will look at the same couple in the restaurant and give an evaluation like this if your friend is a male; "that guy is trying to (accomplish blank)." He is trying to get some specific and measurable result. He may say, "he is trying to get his wife off his back", or, "he is having dinner but has other things to get to afterward."

Stories and responses such as this are the mark of an achiever personality. This type of person will respond well to the technique of "people want things that are hard to get."

A woman friend who is an Achiever might describe the same scene as the following; "she made dinner plans for the two of them," or; "she wants a night out," or; "she looks busy and has things to do." All of these show that the storyteller has a specific goal in mind, and is reaching to achieve that goal, and it's a personal goal of their own.

The goals of the achiever will always sound personal; even if it's a goal at work they will make it sound as their own. She has some stated measurable goal. The achiever must get it done. Whatever "it" may be. They will be the person in the workplace that just takes a project and runs with it. They will not wait for others, they will do it themselves to accomplish the goal if necessary. These types often make excellent workers, but not great managers because they won't delegate, but will just do the work themselves if others won't chip in.

The third type of person is the power player. We call them the Constituents. This person will always want to be in charge. They will use the word I a lot in their stories of what is going on. I, I, I. This characteristic often makes good management material, as they will take charge and delegate responsibilities to get a project done. They will take chances and tend to think outside the box for solutions. They will also respect authority figures, which is one key approach we will use to quickly build rapport with this type of person.

These people will look at that same couple in the restaurant and say things like: "I would do this and this and this," or, "He took charge and told her they were going out to eat," or, "She told him we are going out and he had no choice." Expressions like this infer power and "I." It's all about them. They won't mention the family needs, or the wife's feelings; they will talk as though they are the subject of the event.

Our fourth characteristic trait that we use here is the Peacemaker. These types have a similar motivation to that of the Caretakers. The most important difference is that the overarching motivation with Peacemakers will be to avoid conflict at all cost. Peacemakers desire above all else to keep those around them happy. Use the "avoid unpleasantness" technique when these characteristic traits are shown.

There is often a secondary trait that shows in an individual as well. Don't get confused; people will usually have one trait that is most dominant. Occasionally the secondary trait will be a close second. In such a case either trait will work and be effective as your focus in building rapport with that person. If the dominant trait is obvious, use the technique for that trait first and most intensively. The more tests you do on a person the more obvious it will become as to what the best course of action is for that individual.

The more scenarios that you ask them to describe, and the longer their answers, the better the information you will have for what approach to use for rapport building. You will find with time and practice that a single scenario and a

30 second answer as to what is going on will be sufficient for you to start identifying people's individual traits. I usually ask, "Why?" when someone is telling me their story. It can be a short 15 second story, and they answer the "why" and I have them pegged very accurately. With practice you will learn to do the same.

The best way to learn to identify these character traits is to start with people that you know very well. Get your friends and relatives, and get them to act as your test subjects. You likely already know what characteristic they are, so take notes and see what kind of answers they give you. This is the best way to practice and learn accuracy in identifying characteristic traits of this kind. But remember, the person you are asking cannot know the third party, and they cannot know it is a test or how you are measuring it until it's done. If they know you are looking for characteristic traits beforehand, the results may be different.

The other way we can use this information is with the other part of our four cornerstones of building rapport, as discussed in Chapter One. What we know from our little storytelling test will help us with these as well. Look at the traits that they express, and see how they match up to our four cornerstones. For instance, a Caretaker person will not want to talk negatively about other people as a general rule, so the common enemy will not work with them. They will be much more eager to befriend you if you use the "random favors" technique. They will respond wonderfully to that, as they will definitely acknowledge and respect what you did for them, and will instinctively start to like you. The "agreement" technique will often work with this characteristic type as well. The Achiever will respond well to the "siding goals" technique. They will see a goal, it will align with theirs, and they will enjoy the interaction at that level.

For the power player, the Constituent, use the "common enemy" technique. Choose someone who you know to be in charge and making mistakes, and they will jump all over it. You two will hit it off quickly and effortlessly by using that technique with a Constituent personality type.

CHAPTER 7
Engage Right Brain

One reason Behavioral Programming works better than the other systems out there is because it's organic. This means that it works completely naturally with the way our brains work, and with the way our desires and happiness are generated. They are generated emotionally. We won't get into the physics and chemicals behind this; we're focusing solely on emotional brain characteristics that affect behavior and its modification. One reason behind all of this working is that emotions are not a logical process. They're feelings generated in the right side of the brain. This is where we are doing all of our work because emotions will dictate how we feel about something and will then generate a behavioral response to it.

With this in mind, you always want to engage the right side of the brain during the process of programming. This is done by having the person feel things, not think things. For example, you're programming a person, so you want to ask them questions and make statements about how they feel, not what they think. Ask, "How do you feel about that?" instead of, "What do you think about that?" The thinking proposal will engage the left side of their brain and they'll process the information logically, thinking about it and analyzing it.

We want them to "feel" what we are saying. This whole book is focused on making people feel good. You can't reason your way to a good feeling. You and your friends have tried it many times. You tell yourself, "I shouldn't feel bad about that," and your friends have said, "Don't let them get to you, it doesn't matter." It doesn't work does it? It won't work because your left brain cannot process and override the emotions from the right side of your brain. You must address emotional issues with the right side of the brain to get the best effect.

Behavioral Programming is designed to work strictly with the right side of the brain. Engage a person's emotions when you talk and they'll feel what you're saying, and thus it will have a greater impact and last longer. Think about this; how many times has someone tried to convince you of something and it really all seamed to make sense, but you didn't do it because it didn't "feel right?" We have all done this countless times in our lives.

You have certainly known people who are emotionally attached to people that absolutely abuse them and are bad for them. Any common sense would tell them to get out of that relationship. It doesn't make any logical sense that they would stay with that person, but they do. This is because the emotional right side of the brain is more influential. This is why your parents cannot "arrange" a marriage for you. It would make complete sense to do so logically because of their status, income, family lineage, looks, etc. But you wouldn't want to marry that person because you're not emotionally attached. Emotions will nearly always win over logic. That's how we are programmed.

So when trying to influence someone by using Behavioral Programming, always use emotional language to get them to feel your input, and the programming will take hold. It's like a wire plugged right into their subconscious, running code to their brain, programming them for specific behavior by engaging the right side of the brain.

Another advantage to using the right side of the brain is that their imagination will add good details to what is actually happening. For instance, when programming someone, you can occasionally leave out details of certain things, as their emotions will insert what they want it to be. If you simply explain every detail to them, they'll draw your picture in their head of what you're saying by your specific description using the left side of their brain. If you give fewer details to them, they'll use their right brain to fill in the details according to how they want to imagine it. This will be much more pleasant for them, as we all have our own little things that we like that someone else may not.

An example of this is when you read a book. You have to fill in all of the colors, faces, background, etc. when you read it. Then when you watch the movie you're disappointed because it's not how you pictured it. So be the book, give the pertinent details and let their mind fill in the rest of the picture with what makes them happy, and this will get them emotionally attached to what you're saying.

CHAPTER 8
Reticular Formation

Reticular Formation is how your brain filters out non-essential information. A perfect example of this is when you buy a new car. You drive your car home and notice fifty cars just like yours on your first day with it. This is your RF. Another great example is when you spend the night in a strange place. You'll hear all of the noises that you don't have at your own home. If you're sleeping near a railroad track you'll definitely hear the train as it passes by. The locals there no longer hear the train go by as their RF has filtered out that information. The sound of the train is non-essential to them and therefore their brain won't bring it to their conscious thinking.

The RF is a filter. It filters out the things that we don't need to process (cognitively think about) throughout our daily lives. You can program your RF to pay attention to whatever you desire, but most people have no idea what it is or that they can alter this at all.

What Behavioral Programming does with RF is learn how to use it to program behavior and attention modification. You now know that the person you're talking to is using their Reticular Formation. With this in mind, you can program people to pay more attention to you and to really listen when you talk.

In another chapter we talked about how people won't notice or give any special attention to common, everyday, mundane behavior. Whether it's using LOL, or asking, "How are you?" these things are so common that our RF will barely process them to conscious thought. This won't get anyone's attention, as we see and hear it too many times each day for it to mean anything to us. Your RF is   calibrated to your wants and desires, to things that make you happy. We are going to appeal to a specific individual, not the masses.

This is another key difference in Behavioral Programming versus all of the other influence systems out there. Other systems are based on the masses, things in common to everyone, and no one in particular. Behavioral Programming is based on the individual, and what adds value to them and makes them happy. As you speak to someone, really listen to them and do some initial profiling to see what they are truly interested in. You can really get your point across and gain rapport by interacting with them consciously. We do this by figuring out what their interests are, and then use that theme to get our point across.

For instance, you meet someone at lunch and notice they're wearing a NASCAR t-shirt. You want to build rapport, so you talk about racing. You let them passionately tell you about their favorite driver and the action of last week's race. You then try to explain to them what you do for a living, and why it is important. You will use racing as an analogy for your explanation. You talk about how the pit crew is essential, although no one knows their names, or how important the tires and fuel are, or the suspension to enabling the driver and car to win a race. He will immediately understand what you're saying, and rapport will be built because those are all things that are on his "radar." His RF pushes all of those things he is passionate about to his conscious thought, and you are included in that now.

Reticular Formation is a brain filter, it filters out all of the things you don't need to pay attention to or care about. To get the person to care about what you're saying, you simply program them in a way that their brain will accept it and pay attention. All you have to do is learn what words or subjects are not filtered out by their RF, and make them part of your interaction.

They will truly be engaged in the conversation and actually take interest. Because of this they'll bond with you and rapport will be established. They'll also remember and be able to recall your conversation and the time you spent with them. These are all things that don't normally happen when you first meet someone new.

What normally happens is, someone introduces you, you feel obligated to talk to them, you do so briefly and disengage from the conversation at the first available opportunity. Neither you or they remember each other's names much less made any kind of connection. This is because you really weren't listening to what they were saying. You didn't care. But if they would have talked about your favorite hobby, then you would have actually enjoyed the conversation and taken a valid interest in what they were saying.

Neither one of you pursued a route through the other's RF. Almost nothing they said stuck with you or gained your interest because you really didn't register and process what they were saying. The RF acts as a sentry to their conscious mind and friendship zone. To get past this, you must engage it. Find that one thing that sparks them and they will be plugged in to what you are saying. To get past the RF sentry you can do many things.

Your appearance and dress are also ways to their conscious mind. People who dress out of the ordinary get attention. In fact, that's why most people do it. The psychology behind that is for another book, but suffice it to say that people dress "out of the box" for attention. They do this because it works. You do notice them. Whether you had good or bad thoughts about them doesn't matter, what matters is that you noticed them.

Now, with this in mind we don't need to dress crazy or outrageously, we just need to have one thing that is different than the norm to get us past the sentry. It could be the color of your eyes to the type of shoes you are wearing, something about you makes you stand out and look different than the rest of the crowd. This jumps you right past the guard and into their conscious. You are now on their radar.

If you pay attention, in almost every major US city the norm is black. Everyone wears black. Pants, shoes, shirts, coats, yoga pants, etc.; most every person in the city has on black. It wouldn't take much of a color to differentiate yourself and get noticed by the conscious mind. Anything you do that is out of the norm or baseline will get you attention and you'll be noticed.

So you use that conscious awareness of this to engage them with a conversation that doesn't get caught by the filter (RF). Your words and actions must register with them to get them to engage you and to make your interaction meaningful and memorable. Do this by learning to get past their RF and into their conscious thought.

SECTION 3: CODING BASICS
Reticular Formation

This is what you need to know in order to set the programming code in their brain effectively. These are things to remember while you are running code to modify others behavior.

CHAPTER 9
Scorecard

Your relationship with a person is a sum total of the positive and negative experiences with that person. For instance, every time you greet someone and smile that registers as one good experience with that person. And everything has a point or value system. So a smile and a hello might be worth, let's say, five points. You may have lunch with that person and that may be 20 positive points.

Not every interaction or experience is worth the same number of points. We see this all the time when we talk to someone who is divorced. In the beginning the sum total of their experience together was positive. Things may be very good for two years and the relationship is good and strong. Their relationship might have accumulated 10,000 positive points in the first two years.

A few negative points were deducted for small issues and tussles during their marriage but overall it's weighted toward the positive experiences. Now, let's say that at the end of the second year one of them catches the other cheating. With most people cheating has such a high negative point value that it can turn two years and 10,000 positive points into a negative. That's why when you talk to someone who is divorced they would sum up their marriage negatively.

So our goal is to have a positive experience and interaction with people as often as possible, tipping the scales into our positive point total every time we interact with that person. If you start to view your relationships in a sum total point system like this it will help you to see that work must constantly be done to service the relationship to keep it positive and healthy.

Every time we have contact with a person we leave with either a positive or negative sum for that interaction. The negative emotions and feelings tend to have a much higher point value system then the positive ones. So you must be ever mindful to produce a good feeling with every interaction you have.

One thing to note is that over time the point value system with that person will change. The closer you are to someone the more value is put on negative things. For instance if you have a friend with whom you have had a great relationship for 10 years, the cost of lying to that friend is much higher than the cost of lying to someone you just met because of the trust built in the relationship over time. It can take five to seven good experiences to make up for a single negative one.

CHAPTER 10
Brute Force Brain Hacking

Brute force brain hacking is a term I coined to describe the technique of forcibly programming a person's brain to generate your desired response. Simply put, it's using multiple attack strategies simultaneously on a single person to brute force your programming into their head. Any single technique taught in this book can produce the desired results. However, many times one technique will not be enough to override a commitment or desires or notions that are deeply rooted.

To effectively alter a person's behavior quickly, efficiently, and thoroughly you should use as many techniques as possible simultaneously. This is termed as brute force hacking because it is a repeated onslaught of code after code after code, programming their brain for a specific response. Although any of these techniques could work on their own, brute force hacking gets the most complete result as it is a thorough bombardment of their system by your coding. Just as a computer brain is programmed with a code, you are programming and reprogramming the human brain with your "code."

When people are born they have very few programmed responses. Nearly every action that a person does is a learned response. No one was born knowing how to interact with others and how to treat people; it was all programmed by someone at some point in their lifetime, much of it when they were young. Behavioral programming is a code for the human brain that mandates specific behavior. Brute force hacking is the way most people were originally programmed to do the action that you're trying to change.

An easy example of this would be your mother forcing the word "no" into your brain. It was repeated over and over along with different stimulus to include tone of voice, slapping your hands, facial expressions, walking away, etc. Your mother successfully brute force hacked the proper response to the word "no" into you.

Instead of slapping people's hands or giving them dirty looks or ignoring them, we're going to brute force a behavior by using multiple strategies on that person consistently.

The more techniques that you use properly on a person at the same time, the faster and better your results will be in behavioral modification. So the two key points to make this work is the code that you're writing, which is made up of the individual techniques discussed in this book, and the use of multiple techniques simultaneously. This is what constitutes effective brute force brain hacking.

CHAPTER 11
Susceptibility

People are more susceptible to programming when they're tired and when a particular situation is out of their control. There are a couple of different factors that come into play that cause this. The first is that when things are out of their control and you propose something, in their mind you appear to know more about the solution than they do.

Sometimes this truly is the case when people are stressed out about something. But you must be careful to make sure that what you're programming them to do is actually the best thing for them. You don't want to betray their trust and take advantage of them in their moment of weakness.

The second part is that their feeling of being out-of-control will automatically assign some authority to you. In their mind, whatever is happening is beyond their control and they can do nothing about it, so when you propose an action it's perceived as coming from someone with authority. At this point they won't resist much of what you were programming them to do.

The same type of thing happens when a person is tired. At this point their mental ability to argue reasonably with you is severely diminished. Most of the time this will equate to them submitting to your programming without any thought of resistance. When people are tired, confused, or just mentally worn down, they lose the desire for complex thinking and solutions for problem solving. Knowing this, we'll be there to provide structured input to program their actions for what they should be doing.

A great example of this may be when your friend is going through a break-up of a serious relationship. At this stage people aren't thinking logically and will often make bad choices about what they should or shouldn't do. They may do rash or inappropriate things when left to their own thought processes. This is where we know we must step in and alter their behavior to something more appropriate and helpful for them.

This is a common tactic used by professionals during interviews and interrogations. Sleep deprivation makes a person much less capable of good thought process and mental resistance. The prime time to program someone with these techniques are when they are most susceptible. We're choosing this time because it's also the time when they make bad choices and need logical and structured input, not because we simply have a mental advantage over them. Use the brute force method keeping in mind to make extra effort when people are most susceptible. This will get the most efficient results.

Sometimes it's the little battles that matter and add up. Some people are more difficult to program than others. These people require consistent work. Your words must be carefully thought out and done with the best timing. Usually the time people are this vulnerable is when they need your influence the most.

Unfortunately this is when others influence them away from the correct actions. Many people may come to prey upon this person at this time; however, with your use of the point system and your Alpha status, you should be the most influential to them by far, pushing them into the correct response. This is an opportunity. Take advantage of the opportunity to influence someone when it is presented.

Most people aren't thinking clear and making the right choices when they are vulnerable. This is a time that you must exert your influence and program them for the needed response and behavior. Everything we're programming them to do is still built upon our two pillars. We aren't taking advantage of the person, only taking advantage of the opportunity to help them when they're the most in need of someone to think clearly on their behalf, and when they're the most likely to accept our input. These may be seen as peak programming hours.

Kelly Alwood

CHAPTER 12
Ethical Manipulation

How would I influence people if I had the ability? What would I do if I could get someone to change? If you achieve success in influencing other's behavior, how would that change your life? These are all questions that most of us would answer in a positive way. Most of us do not have a desire in our hearts to take advantage of people. Your desire, if you could do anything you wanted to, would be to alter people's behavior so that everyone was happy around each other, everyone had value, and that everyone was productive. This is what most of us would do if we had the ability to do it. We would change people for the betterment of themselves and also for our relationships with them.

Influence and manipulation have a bad connotation in our society because of people's prior experience with the popular use of such talents. The majority of books, discussions, and teachings on manipulation are in direct conflict with our two pillars. The majority of influence systems being taught are set up on the basis of deceit and personal self gain. Many of the techniques taught to people about manipulation are rather forceful and tricky and not the most healthy way to influence someone.

Power, money, influence, being an Alpha figure; these are all good things when used for good purposes. The problem in our society is that almost every time you see someone with these abilities it's used for personal gain and to do something unethical. This translates into a problem for most good people as they won't actually try to influence or manipulate someone else because they believe it is wrong. Most ethical or moral people will not read a book on manipulation because of the connotations our society has placed upon it and they don't want to be associated with that. The problem therefore becomes that the majority of the people performing influence and manipulation techniques are the ones in our society that we don't want to be doing it.

A common example of this is the expression, "Money is the root of all evil." If you believe that money is evil you'll never obtain wealth. If you believe something is bad and you believe you are a good person you'll never seek after those kinds of things.

Everything in behavioral programming is based on our two pillars that ensure ethics and well-being for others, as well as for ourselves, when manipulating and influencing another's behavior. It's about bad stereotypes and connotations. You don't want to be associated with a group with a bad connotation.

Another example is guns. Good people don't want to carry guns because a gun can have a bad connotation to it. The common stereotype for guns put out by the media and our society is that they are bad things used by bad men. And when a bad man with a gun attempts to use that tool on a good person, who is called but the good man with a gun. As with anything in our lives we choose how to use the tools and opportunities that are given us for right or wrong.

Cars are used by policemen, firemen, and paramedics, disaster relief organizations, and mothers with children. Almost every adult in this country drives a car. However, 100% of the people killed by drunk drivers were killed by someone who used a vehicle to kill an innocent person. It is all about how you use the tools and opportunities given you that determines whether it is good or bad. If only the immoral and unethical people in our society learn to influence us what will our world be like? This book is about achieving a healthy success for everyone. Everyone can learn to be influential and change people's lives. Behavioral programming ensures that this is done for the good.

CHAPTER 13
The Off Switch

Body language will interpret your intentions and seriousness. Far too often people's intentions are misrepresented by themselves. Many people will contradict their words with their body language. Think about it like this: someone is pointing a water hose at you with the intention of spraying you. You point your finger at them and say no, but you have a big smile on your face and behave in a joking manner. Your friends will undoubtedly spray you with water.

We must make sure that our body language is aligned with what our words are saying to others. Throughout this book you're learning code that programs the brain for certain behaviors. We must now match our movements to reinforce that. As we are ever conscious of the exact words and order that we use to program people, we must also make sure our body language is consistent with our programming desired for them.

There are two ways to test your consistency. The first is to be a people watcher and to pay attention to everything going on around you and how people interpret their body language. Observe and study the interactions of other people to see precisely what their actions are programming the other person to do. See how they match up or disregard what words they're saying.

The other way is just to use your basic instincts to match your words and make sure you're not being timid. Too often people betray their own sincerity by their physical actions. This is normally the situation when a person is not aggressive or an Alpha by nature. It often occurs when people don't wish to hurt someone's feelings or be seen as too demanding.

The code that we're using to program people's behavior will work, however the coding can be immediately erased if your physical actions are telling them that you aren't serious. Your posture in physical actions will tell the person if your intent is deliberate, sincere, and real. As long as your posture doesn't negate the code you are using to program them you will be fine.

Posture goes hand-in-hand with the tone in your voice. Either one can completely erase or corrupt the behavioral coding that you are programming into them. Posture and tone will simply convey to the person that your words and coding are serious or if they are to disregard them. Both are like an on/off switch in their brain.

Their brain must be on for the coding to enter and take effect. Make sure you have flipped on the coding switch to their brain or all of the code you're writing will be lost.

I'm sure you've noticed this many times. There is always someone in a group that no one takes seriously. When they're taken seriously it's only after several attempts from the others to confirm that they were in fact actually being serious. This is self-inflicted and is caused by their physical actions, posture, and tone of voice flipping off the coding switch, which is normally due to their lack of self- confidence.

SECTION 4: INITIAL INSTALL OR STARTING A FRESH RELATIONSHIP

Start your relationships off right. These are the things you need to know to start a new relationship off healthy. The code in this section will give you the tools to not only start off on the right foot, but also applies to the rest of your existing relationships.

CHAPTER 14
Defining Your Relationships

The first thing we must do in any relationship is define it. This is necessary, as we will use different social rules with different people in our lives. You don't want to interact with your friends as a boss or employee. You also don't want subordinates at work treating you as a friend. These rules are specific to the behavior we desire to generate from individual interactions.

To activate a certain behavior, you'll use programming language that controls how they interact with you. You must carefully consider how you want to interact with them. This will dictate the methods used. You must decide if your relationship will be defined as professional, personal, or casual.

Once you've set the tone for the relationship, you must be consistent. If you aren't, you'll undermine your own work. Don't send mixed signals. You can change relationships after they've been established, however it must be done carefully and precisely. The key is to carefully examine your desired initial relationship and work to build and maintain that throughout all contact.

One must think carefully about how to define each relationship. You'll see a consistent theme throughout this book, and that is to always think through your actions completely. This sounds simple enough, but as we move further along you'll see how every small detail programs a response from the other person. You're constantly giving out stimulus through words, body language, and presence, generating a response, even unconscious programming, from the other person whether you realize it or not. So from this point forward, you need to be very specific in what you say, how you say it, and the words your body is saying.

Let's define a work relationship. We must be specific and categorize them into one of three groups - coworker (an equal), boss, and subordinate. The standard relationship with a boss is something that has been screwed up and misunderstood by just about everyone out there. This is because people aren't aware of the rules. Just as we're bound by the laws of physics, we're also bound by social laws. Not merely rules, these laws will have adverse effects on our relationships if we break them.

Several methods of interaction are common with a boss. We usually see all of them presented in a single office. You have the suck-up, the disrespectful, the "yes man," the lazy one, the rebel, and many more. The most common tactic for those trying to climb the ladder are the suck up, and the hard worker. Unfortunately, these don't work like you think they do. They may seem to work at times, but the boss doesn't see you the way you want him or her to. Most of the time you are labeled as the dependable slave.

What does work is programming your boss to respect you and your talents. We all have talents and abilities that are better than others. We must find the ones that we have that the boss can use. You need to make the boss aware of your special abilities that can benefit them. It may be your flexibility, your creative thinking, your knowledge, or anything else. The suck-ups will always make themselves available. We'll discuss this abuse of time and talent in another chapter. The hard worker will get the boss's attention for sure. But that doesn't mean that they'll get the promotion or any benefit other than keeping their current job.

The boss will move people closer to him or her that they feel comfortable and compatible with. Another person in the workplace is making friends with the boss, and the guy doing the hard work will just be placed under the friend's control. The hard worker won't advance because the boss is not friendly with them. But to make sure the work gets done, they'll keep that person and put them under the control of the boss's friend. If you want the boss to promote you, and bring you up, then you must make a personal relationship with them.

Of course doing great at your job won't hurt, but it certainly isn't a requirement. The boss wants someone that is like them. Someone compatible.

The suck-up may get things done, but the boss will never look to them as equals or even close to equal. They are annoying to just about everyone, including the boss. The boss will keep them around because they are a reliable slave. But the boss will not promote them because they don't like to be around them either.

The boss solution

Make your talents known to the boss. Let them know what an asset you are to the team. Find a way to make your talent magnify your job and add value to the product the company offers. We all have things we excel at. Most aren't willing to give of their talents to help the team, especially when they think it isn't appreciated and acknowledged. At all times, be respectful. At no time will you ever address them casually when others are around. Take a personal interest in the boss and his/her life.

Don't talk about work all the time. Everyone else there does that. Ask them about their family and hobbies and so on. Bring up personal things when you are not around the others and that will set the tone for a different relationship with them. After a while, you'll pick up a different vibe from the boss. When they demonstrate that they have a desire to talk to you on a personal level of some sort, you know you're making progress.

At this point you can test the waters. When no one is around, try speech that is a little less formal and more casual and see what their response is. It may be as simple as you seeing him in the coffee room and drop the Mr. when addressing him. Or you may ask them their opinion on a personal matter of yours.

This will test the waters and let you see how the boss is viewing you currently. If you ask them for advice or opinion, make it very generic and non- consequential. Don't turn it into the Jerry Springer Show by bringing in embarrassing details about your personal life. Maybe pick two vehicles you like and ask them which one they would buy. That gets them into your personal life, but not too deep.

There is a line between being friendly and good to have around, and being a suck-up. Being friendly and personally approachable is good. You may choose to simply stay where you are; good at your job, and not personally involved with the boss. That is also fine. Just keep the rules in mind, and don't cross over back and forth.

This also uses our two pillars. The first pillar is met by us actually bringing our real talents and abilities to bear for the team effort. We also use honesty in our approach of getting personal with the boss. There is nothing deceitful about what we're doing here.

The second pillar is met by both parties getting ahead. First, if we choose to keep everything professional as it has been, then we both benefit from a good working relationship. No surprises. We give and get respect as do they. If we choose to get more personal, then we'll both benefit from a real friendship that will last and take us both further in success in the business.

How do we deal with subordinates? Again, we must be consistent. You need to realize the pecking order in the work place, and then stick to it for the most part. If you have people beneath you at work, you want to establish a good working relationship with them. Everyone likes people who are nice, so that one is a given. Being nice and being a pushover are two very different things. It's much easier to get subordinates to do what you want when they like you. So you can always be nice.

To keep them in line and not allow them to take advantage of you, and to maintain order you must also be firm. If you're open for others opinions and views, then let them know you will listen but that you will make a decision and that your decision is final. If you don't want input from them, then make that known right up front. Explain to them nicely, but firmly, that you simply want them to do what is asked of them, and don't wish to discuss it with them.

You can never tolerate a subordinate speaking to you like a friend. You aren't friends. You are coworkers and you are over them. You can be nice to them without being friendly. Friendly is often shown by being chatty, gossiping, or discussing personal issues not related to work. You never want to be friends with subordinates at work.

Outside of work is a whole different world which we will discuss in detail later. In the workplace, you must maintain your control over the work force you command. Never let anyone speak to you as if talking to a friend. This will start to program them into thinking there is another level to this relationship and change their behavior towards you. Keep it as formal and professional as needed for them to treat you like the boss.

You'll know when you have let your guard too low as the people below you will show it with speech and deed. They'll start to back talk or argue with you or they'll not get the work done, all because they now believe that you are more friends than coworkers and that you won't force them to comply as you did before.

When this happens, you must immediately address the disrespect and make clear that they are below you. This should reset the behavior, as long as you keep it consistently work-based and no more personal, friendly atmosphere. If you have a subordinate at your work place, keep it that way. That is how life is. There is nothing wrong with that. We all have a boss and most people have someone under them. Just keep it formal and consistent.

Outside of work we have a lot more choices of categories to place people. Again, we must be consistent. That doesn't mean that we can never change our relationships with people. Upgrade or downgrade them. This rule means that we have defined to ourselves what we wish the relationship to be, and then we program them appropriately for that purpose. For instance, we may have an acquaintance, a friend of a friend that was introduced to us and the group. We will plug them into the group into their natural pecking order, most likely starting at the bottom.

We may find that we really like this person and want to be good friends. That is perfectly fine, we just need to acknowledge that that is our new desire and program them for their new role. What we don't want is to program them for a friend role if we desire to keep them at arms length as an acquaintance. We can't send mixed signals. This will benefit neither of us. They'll not get our friendship, and we'll be annoyed by this person trying to be our friend.

We must look at the proper structure of every relationship. We must first define it, how we want it to be, and then structure our behavior to program the person to fall into that slot. If you want a real friendship, then you must structure it correctly.

Let's say you have a friend of the opposite sex. Let's say you are immediately attracted to them from the start. But you start off trying to be this person's friend. Your actions program this person to be a friend. You determined early on that you were going to be friends. That's fine, but when you later try to alter their perception and behavior as a friend to a boyfriend/girlfriend, it will be much more difficult.

If you originally looked at that person and wanted to be more than friends, then you should start the relationship with that approach. Program them to be a great boyfriend or girlfriend right from the beginning. You must be as consistent as possible. Some relationships will change. Some will get upgraded and some downgraded with time. However, we need to keep them as stable as possible. Your status in the group may change as well.

We'll discuss the Alpha dynamics in detail and how all of that works in another chapter. But for the most part, we want strong consistent relationships that last and are drama free. Drama comes from inconsistency.

When you have decided in what category to place someone, then you must, from that point forward, make sure that your actions are consistent with the desired result. Don't go back and forth. If you've decided to be friends with someone, then you must treat them like that all the time. You must also demand from them the same behavior.

To keep things working correctly, you must make them keep with consistent behavior towards you as well. When a person steps out of their designated role, you must swiftly challenge that as to not let their behavior continue off course. If their behavior is not challenged immediately, then their actions will get more and more out of line with time.

For example, let's say that you have a good friend. You're close and joke around a lot with each other, just normal friendly kidding around. One day your friend kids around with you in front of other people that aren't close to you. In the other people's eyes, your friend has just disrespected you. They don't see it as two friends joking with each other. It will be perceived by people outside your group of intimate friends as a joke on you, one that is meant for disrespect.

You must immediately correct this behavior in front of everyone. You don't want to disrespect your friend while doing so. That will only encourage what has happened. Instead, a direct challenge to that person such as "that wasn't cool" or something similar will get the needed response. With this your friend will see that you feel slighted by his comment and he will apologize. All is well now. The others around you observing this will see that your friend didn't mean it the way they took it.

If this situation is not immediately corrected, then likely the other people around you will see a chance to jump in with their own comment about you, teaming up with your friend's statement against you. You'll then be mad at your friend, and really start to dislike the third party. No one wins in this scenario.

So anytime someone steps out of their role, they should be immediately challenged. How harsh or gently you correct someone is up to you, and different situations and people will require different corrections to get results. Usually it's safe to start with less aggressive language. A gentle reminder is all that is needed most of the time.

CHAPTER 15
You Teach People How to Treat You

This is something that I discovered by observing different people's relationships and trying to figure out why some people had zero respect at work or home or in their "group of friends," and why others were worshiped and revered. What I noticed was that each person thought of themselves the same way that people treated them. This is one extremely important part of behavioral programming. This alone will change your relationships forever.

People will treat you exactly as you demand of them and teach them that you should be treated. If you let someone make you the center of a joke, they'll continue to do so. It will also change the perception of everyone around you. Everyone that was present at the event will treat you as the butt of a joke. An Alpha figure will immediately go on the offense, and let everyone there know that they aren't to be made fun of. If you follow the other programming rules while doing this, you'll come out as the Alpha figure.

I was on a long road trip last year with a friend of mine. He was on the phone with a girl for quite some time, then would hang up and start telling me how disgusted he was. He was having an issue with this female friend and respect. He is an instructor, and a friend of his, who was also one of his students, was treating him differently that she had ever done before. He couldn't understand why. He was quite confused and irritated. The girl had started dating another instructor, and was treating him like he was now a second class instructor. And so our talk began.

I told him, "You teach people how to treat you." I explained to him that this girl was disrespecting him because he was breaking all of the rules. He taught her that it was ok to treat him like that. He was a bit confused so I went on to explain.

I told him that every time she called, he answered and listened to her rant before he got a word in. Then he would proceed to try to explain himself to her, and defend his position, making sure not of offend her. I told him this will never work. He had taught her that he is waiting for her call, will answer the phone and talk any time that it's convenient for her, and that he will listen to her because she is more important. His eyes raised, and he got a funny look on his face.

I said, "Do you trust me? Do you trust my advice about behavioral programming?"

He answered, "Yes." Continuing he said, "I've seen you pull 180's on people's thoughts, and have watched you program people many times. I know you know how."

So I told him, "Then do exactly what I say, and by the end of the day, she will be eating out of your hand again."

"What do you think I should do?" he asked me.

I said the next time she calls, don't answer the phone. "And then what?" he asks.

"Don't pick up the phone all day. She'll be mad and irritated with you for the next couple of hours. Then she'll start to wonder why she can't keep your attention. Then she'll start to text. She'll crave your acknowledgment of her. It'll drive her nuts, that you don't make time for her. She'll start to text nasty things at first to try to bully or guilt you into talking to her. But in her mind she'll start to wonder if she still has that grip on you.

Then the texts will get more mild. She'll say something nice. After still not getting a reply, she'll then start to feel inferior and completely inadequate to you. Then she'll act concerned. She'll text and leave voice mails asking if you are ok.

That is a tactic to get you to acknowledge her, because people simply can't ignore concern. It breaks all social rules and etiquette.

At this point we'll be 5-6 hours into the session of reprogramming. You'll send her a very brief and direct text. 'I'm not happy with your attitude, I'll contact you later.' After this, she'll have a complete change of attitude. She'll accept her spot as Beta, and you again as Alpha, and beg for forgiveness. She'll apologize, and then let you know that she is at your service."

He asked me if I really thought this would work.

I told him, "Of course it will work. Don't deviate from my directions.

The correspondence came exactly as I told him it would. It took a couple times stopping him from straying off the route I had laid out. But he did just as I said. And everything unfolded precisely as I had predicted. By the end of the day, she had resumed her place as the good student, and he was now again captain of the ship. He had taught her to treat him that way. He told her through his actions and choice of words that it was acceptable to treat him that way. She simply needed programming on how to treat him. He acted, and she responded as programmed.

If you establish yourself as an Alpha, and keep doing so, then you'll be treated as one. It doesn't mean that you're THE Alpha of the group however. Imagine this; you are a qualified but "new guy" on the job. You certainly aren't going to be THE Alpha figure in the office. There is obviously someone above you in everything. Pay, seniority, respect, knowledge, experience, not to mention the owner, and the "boss" who has been there forever. They will remain Alpha.

However, you can program everyone there that you are also an Alpha figure, including the "boss," or manager, or higher ups. You demand respect as superior to everyone else there, even though it's your first day on the job.

You can't be arrogant; instead you must do this by following the guidelines in the other chapters of this book. You'll be treated as an Alpha, even though you really aren't. You'll demand the respect of your superiors, and since you have the respect of the higher-ups everyone else will be programmed to treat you as an Alpha.

People will treat you the way you train them to. Plain and simple. If you become a pushover wussy, then you've taught them to do that. Your actions have conditioned others as to how they'll treat you. Now knowing this, think about how other people treat you. I have friends that must help everyone out. A great hearted guy, but he has trained others to take advantage of his kindness. Every single day of his life, someone calls on him to do a chore or favor for them. And he does. He has taught them to do that.

How many times have you told someone that you care about to "just tell them no?" We all have. We can all see when someone is being taken advantage of. So we advise them to stop allowing it to happen. The problem is, you must do it correctly. That's why most people keep doing it. They don't want to "make someone mad" or "hurt someone's feelings."

We've all seen this within our circle of friends time and time again. And your friend is correct. To simply tell them "no" would most likely severely alter their relationship with that person. However, that's exactly what we're trying to do. We're not trying to end the relationship, but rather to alter it and make it better for everyone in it. So think about this the next time someone disrespects you, tries to take advantage of you, or otherwise treats you in a way that you don't like. You have trained them to do it. You can also train them not to.

If someone you know says something disrespectful or degrading to you, it's because they have done it before, or witnessed someone else do that to you and the action went unchallenged. They challenged your Alpha status, and you didn't respond to the challenge. But remember, everything we discuss in this book is for the good. We can't lash out and make people angry, or you just lose the relationship with that person. We're not looking to drop people off of our list of friends and acquaintances. We're simply looking to improve our relationship with them.

So how we gain respect from our peers is critical. If someone is joking around and makes you part of the laugh, you can simply say "that's not funny." It's very direct, it will get an immediate response, and it corrects the behavior. The person will immediately apologize and you will accept. The situation will be over, and it won't be repeated.

The general rule is: when you don't like what someone is doing to you, let them know it can't continue. Whether it be asking you for money frequently, or not asking your opinion, speak up and make it known. The person's behavior won't change if you don't stop it. They won't stop it on their own. You've taught them by your inaction that this behavior is acceptable to you. You let them get away with it and that tells them to keep doing it.

The need to alter the way people treat you is big. As mentioned earlier, mutual benefit is needed for every relationship to work. So, if you're unhappy because someone treats you badly, then you really don't have a friendship, you have a battered relationship.

You need to demand to be treated in a way that makes you feel good around that person. You also need to be the friend that makes them feel good. If you aren't treated the way you would like to be, it's because you taught that person that it's ok to treat you that way. The sooner you demand respect, the easier the transition will be to a friendlier relationship with that person.

Pay attention to details. When you're in a friendship, often we joke around with each other. That's friendly and normal. However, you must pay attention to the jokes and the way they are made. Pay attention to how they answer the phone when you call. Notice how they greet you when you get together. As your value to the relationship decreases in their eyes, these little details will give it away.

Take notice of any change in the normal healthy behavior that they always have with you. When this changes, your status with them has changed. Sometimes it's a shifting of Alpha status, and sometimes it's because someone else has started to replace the value that you add to that person.

Relationships are always evolving. New people are always being added and subtracted from every peer group. When this happens, the dynamics of the group can change. Where you once stood as the Alpha of the group in (insert your best quality or skill), the new guy coming in may be seen as having more of your value than you do, setting you in a lower status of your pack.

Let's say you're the funny guy in the group. Your friends love to hear your jokes and you can always come up with something witty at the right time. That's your big value to the group. You may have other contributions as well, but that's what the group really takes from you the most. When another guy comes into the group and is funnier than you are, that will demote your status as a result of your value being lowered. His jokes are new and fresh as compared to yours, as you've been friends for a long time.

When this happens you'll notice a change in how you're treated by the group. At this point you must remind the person or group how you are to be treated. You need to make sure that you're still treated the same way as before, or you friendship with that person or group will crumble. All parties need to be happy.

As people grow in character they get stronger. As we go through life we should all be gaining talents, knowledge, and experience. Because of this, a person who was the Beta previously now becomes the Alpha.

Let's say you were the smart one of the group. Everyone close to you looked to you for answers and knowledge. That was the key to your Alpha status. That's the value that you added to your group. Let's say a friend gets a new job that everyone agrees is pretty prestigious. It includes a big pay raise and title. He or she may now be looked at by the group as the new smart one. You may have been the smartest one, but you quit developing that value and someone else surpassed you. Now your status and value with the group has changed.

If you pay attention to the details you'll see this developing. You'll start to notice the group asking the other person questions that they used to ask you. You'll have two options at this point. First, attempt to keep your status as the Alpha of your value. This means you will have to prove to the group for a while that you're still the best guy at what you do.

Your second option is to give up that value to the better person, and quickly add another value the group lacks. If you used to be the smartest guy in the group, now you may switch to being the toughest guy, or the most dependable person, or even the funniest one in the group.

The key is to always add value so everyone wins. If your value changes, you need to immediately teach people how to treat you with this new value. Demand the treatment you desire because you're still adding value to the whole.

CHAPTER 16
Be Yourself

Everyone is different. It seems at times that everyone around us is trying to be like someone else. This can be productive or detrimental, depending on how we apply it. In a way, we should all try to be like someone else. We should look at those who inspire us, pick out the best attributes that we would like to have, and attain those qualities for ourselves. This doesn't mean that we that we're trying to be someone that we aren't. This means that we're constantly making ourselves a better version of who we currently are. Never pretend to be someone that you aren't. Never pretend to be anything.

In a way, we are all wannabes. We all strive to be something that we aren't. That's perfectly healthy. That's how we grow and change and improve. We aspire to be something that we aren't yet. So we're constantly improving ourselves. The mistake is pretending to be something or someone that we aren't. We're all very different and have something to contribute to someone else's benefit. Part of your value is that you're different.

Far too often people try to pretend to be like someone else to try to fit in or gain attention. The truth is that you can be a value to that person or group by being different. You have talents, abilities, knowledge, and experiences that they don't. People tend to group with people who are like them. However, we aren't clones of each other. Your value or benefit to a person or group are your unique attributes. You can be accepted into a group of people that are nothing like you, simply by offering value.

My friend Troy said to me one day, referring to a computer security training course, "I would rather have a computer geek with taped glasses teach me how to hack a computer rather than another door kicker." He, as you should be, is willing to accept people for their value and talents. That computer nerd with taped glasses will be treated respectfully by these Special Forces operators because he offers them value.

That's the rule. Be who you are. You have value to offer another person. You have talents and abilities that they don't. You don't need to be "just like them" to be accepted. Just be exceptional at what you do. Offer something of value to a person and they will let you in.

One person is always better at a particular thing than everyone else. There can only be one "best." So everyone in the group is probably "best" at something in that group. That's their benefit to the group. You need to find your best attributes, focus on those as your value, and sell that to people. You may be the smartest one in the group. You may be the strongest, the most fit, the funniest, the whatever. Just find your best things and offer those to people. This is a way to be yourself and also be of value to the group.

Too many people try to pretend to be someone that they aren't. This is quickly discovered by people and they won't be accepted any more, as they don't offer value to the group. In fact, they did have value to add, but they didn't offer that, they chose to pretend to be something else.

Program others to respect you by being yourself and demanding respect. You'll be held in high regard by others. What's worse than a loser? A loser that's pretending to be someone special. They're annoying. They drive everyone nuts. Don't be that person. Be yourself, demand respect, offer value, and you'll be held in high regard by those around you.

The way to keep that high esteem that you've earned is to keep making yourself better. Strive to improve yourself always, and you'll continue to add value to other people's lives. This will also build your confidence. Your confidence is a key role in being accepted and respected. When you know who you are, and what your real value is to someone, that will give you the confidence that you need to match your demeanor to your capabilities.

Without confidence others will be slow to respect you. Great self confidence will program others to respect you. That is who you are, a confident, value adding benefit to someone's life.

CHAPTER 17
Appearance

Most people would give you the same advice when advising you how to dress. The common thought is that to make a good first impression you need to be well- dressed. This actually is not the case at all. Your appearance describes your personality and interests. Your appearance is very important and will immediately tell a story about you to the people that you're meeting. Being clean and smelling good with good personal hygiene is a must; however, how you dress is a direct reflection of your personality and interests. It is also an indicator of your Alpha status.

Every day when you're outside of work you wear a uniform. We all wear a uniform that tells others who we are. The type of shoes, type of watch, and the logos on your shirts speak volumes about who you are and what your interests are.

When you're meeting someone for the first time on a personal level, and not looking for a job, you should dress as you normally dress. This will immediately give the other person a strong indicator of who you are right from the start.

If you meet someone for the first time and dress differently than you normally do, the other person may have mixed signals or may not be able to ascertain who you really are. You may put on different clothes and dress a little nicer to meet these people and then two hours into your activity with them it's obvious that your clothes do not match your personality. This is one of the biggest oversights people normally have about relationships and it causes confusion for the other person.

People will immediately look at your dress and base conversations off of that.

For instance, your friend tells you to meet them at your favorite restaurant to introduce you to a new coworker of theirs. So you put on some casual khaki pants and a golf shirt because you assume that is how they will be dressed.

You get to the restaurant and the conversation starts out with interests they are guessing that you have and what you do for a living. You then tell them you are a skydiving instructor and it throws the entire conversation off. Why would a skydiver who normally wears sandals, shorts, and skydiving T-shirts be dressed like this?

The other person will feel embarrassed and awkward that they were that wrong about your personality and posed conversational questions to you that were completely out of line with who you are. Now in their mind they will be wondering why you are dressed that way and will spend the rest of the conversation trying to pinpoint your personality and who you really are. You are giving off mixed signals and it is very confusing to the other person. In an indirect way you're not being honest with them about who you really are. You are in the uniform of someone else and misrepresenting yourself by your appearance. The best thing to do is always be yourself.

Of course, we all have times when we have our relaxed self and our professional or formal self depending on the occasion. However, if it's not a formal or professional occasion we should dress in the uniform that we do everyday.

One thing you'll notice about Alphas is their appearance is quite consistent. They'll dress to their personality and interests, and will normally have something unique that stands out. In a casual setting they'll always wear their uniform of self- identification and it will be quite predictable.

This doesn't mean that they will wear the exact same thing all the time. It means they have a style of dress that is predictable for them and their personality. That thing that is unique about them and their dress, is something you can count on them having, may be different all the time.

The consistency is that they will have something unique in their uniform all the time although the individual item may change.

In the pick-up artist world they call this peacocking. It's something that makes them stand out in a crowd, something that people will notice. An item of their apparel says I am different and I am an Alpha. This may be an unusual type of hat, different kinds of footwear, belts, or other accessories, but you can always count on them having something unique in their apparel. So avoid awkward moments and questions, avoid confusion, and dress as who you are. Wear your uniform that currently portrays you in all casual

situations.

Kelly Alwood

CHAPTER 18
Keywords

These are a set of keywords to avoid using, or to use only in very specific ways and circumstances. The context in which you use a word will program a certain response from people. Let's look at some of these key words.

"Hope"

Don't use the word "hope." This word generates negative thoughts towards you. It registers as doubtful expectations of your capabilities. By you using the word "hope" in reference to yourself, you've just placed all the negative connotations on you, and other's respect and expectations for you is lowered. On the contrary, when you use "hope" directed at someone else it means "expected." For instance, "I hope I will get it done" and "I hope you would get it done." The first one suggests that you most likely or probably won't get something done. You're telling them not to expect you to perform as planned. In the second example we see a phrase we have used many times. In every case we meant "expect" not hope. Every parent has looked at their kids and said "I hope you cleaned your room," implying that it was expected of them. "Hope" when directed at others implies expected compliance.

"Sir"

This is a statement of submission. Whenever someone gives you this respect take it and run with it. Don't act surprised that someone addressed you with respect. Don't direct people not to use that title when addressing you. This is a mistake most people make. Most people don't like the term used with them, usually because they don't feel as though they deserve the honor from someone else. When you correct someone for using "Sir" to address you, you make it clear to them that they don't need to show you any respect. You tell them that you're no better than they are. You reject the honor they bestowed upon you.

Whenever possible, don't voluntarily use this term with someone else. It's not a bad thing to show respect, however the use of this term won't put you in a place of friends or of equals. It will always place you lower when you use this term addressing another. Respect is earned, not freely given. Friends don't call each other "Sir" in the company of friends or unofficial situations.

"Sorry"

Don't apologize for things or other people. This places the guilt on you, a shared responsibility for what has happened. Apologizing puts you in a submissive position as the other person has now loan sharked you. You owe them because you're somehow partially at fault. Ever since you were a small child, you were told to go tell someone "I'm sorry," for what you had done. "I'm sorry," is a statement of accepted guilt. An example of this might be "I'm sorry he lied to you," or "I'm sorry you had a bad day."

The person's first response when you say those things is always, "It's not your fault." That's because you took responsibility for it when you apologized for it. The person is already having a rough time obviously, so don't associate yourself with that thought. It'll register with them that you are somehow connected, when in fact you just feel sorry for them. You aren't sorry to them. It had nothing to do with you.

There are many ways to express this other than using the term "I'm sorry." The proper thing to do is to place yourself in the situation with them. Share their pain or sorrow with your words, don't share the guilt of the act.

For instance, instead of saying, "I'm sorry for your loss," you can say, "I miss them too," or, "This is a hard time for us." Putting yourself in with them will make them not feel alone in going through whatever situation they are dealing with. It makes them feel as though you are going through the tough time with them. "I'm sorry," makes them feel as though they are facing it alone, as you are looking at it from the outside.

"Guess"

It 's always a bad idea to use the word "guess." Most people say it all the time.

You are asked if "this or that would be ok" and you often times answer "I guess." This demonstrates a submissive attitude. It registers to the other person that you don't have a better thought of your own. Their brain will remember the submissive behavior and their tactics will adjust accordingly.

Most of the time we do have an opinion on the matter, but we are afraid to say "no." We're put on the spot, didn't see the question coming, and don't want to offend anyone with a "no" answer. "I guess" is our way of saying "I don't really want to, but I can't say no, so I'll do it."

The other person is usually in a bind and that's why they phrase the question that way. They knew before they asked that it would be a hardship, or at a minimum, undesirable for you to say yes. They purposefully phrase the question that way because they know your programmed response is favorable to them. "Would that be ok?" That is how most of these questions start out. Very seldom can a person say no to a question phrased that way. "I guess," is the beginning of unproductive responses because they normally go like this; "I guess I can watch her for you. I'll just stay home," or, "I guess you can borrow that. I wasn't going to use it for a while anyway."

The "I guess" set you up for submissive failure, and then the rest of your response sealed the deal. You went on to explain to them why it was ok for them to push this on to you, and that you can adjust for their demands. This is neither healthy for them or you. They've programmed you to submit to this phrase, and take advantage of you knowing that you don't want to do this. You're obviously not happy with them roping you into this. What needs to be said is "no."

Keeping in mind our rules of explanation, we tell them we can't do this or that because of this or that. One of the best ways out of this is, probably something that you have heard said to you many times, "I would but....". This is an easy way to tell someone no. It implies that "I would like to help you, but I cannot for (this very good reason)." By using the word "can't" or "cannot" because (blank), it pretty much ends the rebuttal from them. If you don't use the word "can't" or "cannot" it leaves it open to suggestions from them. They'll come up with an idea why or how you can do this for them.

"Try"

This is another term that works both ways. When used towards someone it registers as "expected." I'm sure we've all heard this a million times from our mothers and teachers.

Mom: "Is your room clean?" You: "No, I can't make my bed." Mom: "Try."

Teacher: Is your math done?" You: "No, I can't figure it out." Teacher: "Try."

In every case that word "try" is directed at someone else it registers in the other persons head as "expected." There really is no "try" intended, they actually intend or expect you to do it. When we use the term directed at ourselves, it registers as "probably not going to happen" to the other person.

A typical example is, "Are you going out with us tonight?"

"I'll try to make it."

Everyone knows that that means you really don't want to and/or you're not going to put effort into making it happen. The problem is that the other person asked you the question hoping that you would say yes. When you answer them with "try," it registers in their head as a negative response.

It turns out to be worse than just saying no because they will get a second bad feeling when they later ask you again. "Are you going out with us tonight?"

"I'll try to make it."

Then later that night when the crew is going out, that person will call or text you and ask again, and again their hopes will be up that you will say yes. When you tell them, "No, I can't make it because... (insert typical bad excuse you have used)." They're disappointed a second time with the same event. It would be better for you to say no up front if you don't think you can.

Whether it is because you don't want to or because the situation is not prudent, you normally have a good idea if you're actually going to show or not. So be upfront and honest and cut back on the disappointment that you make them feel. Remember, it's all about the total sum number.

"Anyway"

This is a word that does little good. You should probably find another word to use than "anyway." This word will not program others to respect you. This word will program people to not listen to you and/or not want to talk to you.

Using "anyway" will nullify everything you just said before that. It translates into "forget it" when referring to yourself. You get done explaining some details of a story and then say, "Anyway, she's fine now," or whatever it was.

That's all that the person will remember. It's like a brain scrub. You wiped their hard drive of the information you just downloaded to them. Not only won't they remember any of the details that you just told them, but they'll actually view your comments as irrelevant. People will start to not really listen when you talk. They will wait for the "punch line" of your comment as you will use "anyway" and sum it all up for them. There really is no reason to pay attention to your whole story because you will give the important details at the end.

You've programmed them to do this when you speak. When referring to others, it says "I'm not interested," or, "I don't believe you." Someone says to you "I can't wait to see the game tonight," and you reply, "Anyway, how did your exam go today?"

Normally we use "anyway" as a way to abruptly change a subject to one that we actually care about at the time. Depending on what the other person said, when you say, "Anyway....," that person knows immediately that you don't care about what they just said. You don't even dignify or recognize that they even spoke when you say, "Anyway." This obviously programs people to not want to talk to you. This could be a good technique to use if you really have no desire to ever have a conversation with that person again. For everyone else, you should avoid using "anyway."

CHAPTER 19
Word Selection

Be very specific in your selection of the words you use. When someone needs something and is looking for a favor, you tell them "I have it," or, "I have one." This communicates two different things to the person in need. "I have one," means I personally own one and I'm waiting for you to ask to use it because you're in need and you owe me now. "I have I,t" tells the person that you not only have one, but that you have what they're looking for, they're somehow entitled to it, and it's not so much that they owe you for it. You now just obligated yourself to deliver it because you have it.

We'll discuss the order we put our words into in a different chapter. You need to be very conscious of everything you say to everyone. You can no longer go on auto reply.

Much of what we do and say every day is an automated answer taught to us by society. Almost everyone we have interaction with gives us the same reply as the last person we talk to. As a matter of fact, when asks a question in a greeting most people will not wait for nor even expect an actual reply. It's simply something people have learned to say to others. We need to break this habit to better our relationships and program people to what we expect and to how we will treat our relationship with them.

The next time someone asks you a question think about your reply completely before answering them. Think about the words you will choose and how that will translate in their brain into some kind of programming. You need to be very conscious of your word choices and be very specific in which words you use as they are all code to program the other person's brain for a certain and specific response. Too often we simply just throw out a reply on autopilot without thinking about what we really told them and how they will actually interpret that.

One example is a friend who stops by unannounced wanting your time. They may want your help with something, they may want to go out, or they may just want to talk. Whatever the case they notice that you are busy and cannot donate any time right now. The typical response from your friend is, "Can I help?" They were on auto reply and your auto response to their question is normally, "No, I can get it." This is caused by two factors. The first factor is that your friend came to you in need of something and they don't really desire to help you. The second factor is because they're your friend they had to generate that auto response asking if you need help. "Can I help?" is a question people ask as a formality and don't expect an answer in the affirmative; they really don't want to help you but feel they must ask you anyway. That specific question tells the other person that they really are not interested in helping and you should decline their offer. If you really desire to help someone you would ask them "What can I do?" or "Tell me what to do." When you hear that from someone you immediately suspect they are sincere in their desire to help you. It's all about what you say.

Your word choices will make a huge difference in delivering your actual meaning and intent. Everything you say will be interpreted in their head and will program them for a response. Don't rush to answer peoples questions or make comments and statements before you have thought specifically about what you're saying to them. There are very few times when you should make a statement that you haven't anticipated exactly how the person will respond.

CHAPTER 20
Packaging

It's all about the packaging. It's how you phrase the question. For instance, don't tell someone, "Hey, I hear you have this or that for sale." Instead say, "I hear you are trying to sell this or that." That simple distinction reframes what their condition is, a condition of power or a condition of need. The way you phrase a question or statement will program that person to view the discussion or question at the angle you want them to.

To use influence on someone you must be in a position of dominance. With every question that you ask there is a way to phrase it that puts the other person in a more submissive frame of mind so you'll be more influential in the desired outcome. There's a line that can be crossed, however; if you phrase a question with such dominance that it shocks the other person this will immediately minimize your influence. Giving the person an ultimatum is an example of this. When the question is phrased this strongly, one side of the response will normally be aggressive resistance. You'll never score positive points by pushing someone into a corner and forcing them to decide between bad and worse. So pay particular attention to how you phrase your questions, and whether your question put them in a more needy spot rather than a position of power and options.

Another example could be asking your friend, "What are you doing tonight?" This gives the person many options and the open ability to not include you. If you simply package the question differently it will generate a predicted response; "Do you want to have dinner with me tonight?" When you phrase the question this way it puts them in a spot of saying yes, or being rude and disappointing you. "Do you want," makes the person verbalize upfront that they do not desire to be with you or do something for you. The only way for a person to get out of a "do you want" question is to say, "I can't."

When your question is directed to a friend they will rarely tell you "I don't want to," rather, they will normally say, "I can't." Immediately following this and normally attached to it is their defense and explanation of why they cannot do it. So you know upfront when you phrase the question, "Do you want to ___?" if the person does not want to they will say, "I can't because___." You need to have already anticipated what their excuse will be, explain to them that you have a solution for that, and that you are depending on them. If you have built influence, racked up positive points, and they owe you favors, then they will have a very difficult time saying no to your request.

CHAPTER 21
Dos and Don'ts

Do:

Do believe in what another person says. This means that you're going to put some faith in this person and believe that they believe what they're saying. This does not mean that you just believe everything everyone tells you. What you must do is listen to the person talk. Realize that, whether right or wrong in our opinion, they believe what they're saying. If it turns out later that they were lying to us, then we'll discover this quickly and know that their intentions from the beginning were deceitful. Most of the time this isn't the case. The key here is to listen to them. We may not agree on what they are saying, but we understand that this is their stance or belief or opinion on that particular matter, and we must respect that to be a good friend.

If you don't listen to what someone is saying, then you run a high risk of offending them at some point. It would be better to listen in the beginning and find out that you're too different to be friends and let it go softly than to have it blow up later. Let's say that the person you just met is a religious person. You listen to them and take mental note of what they're saying. You believe them. Now you'll have information about them that'll help you communicate more effectively. This insight lets you know that your language during a conversation should be without cursing, as an example. This will help you avoid making offensive mistakes that will negatively shape their opinion of you. They will be comfortable talking to you, and enjoy your time together.

This may seem like a small point, but it will score you big points emotionally as the brain recognizes sincerity. It's very difficult to pretend to listen, care, and believe if you actually don't. More often than not, your true actions and thoughts will be realized by the other person. You can always tell when you're talking to someone and they don't believe you. So look at the person speaking, listen to what they say, and believe that they believe what they are saying. This will register in the brain as a feel good emotion.

The second part to this is belief in what you say. You have to be committed and believe in what you say. The words you choose, your body language, and other things will tell the other person that you don't really believe in what you're saying. It will register to them as dishonesty. And it is. If you don't really believe it, don't say it.

A common mistake is to play "devil's advocate," to take an opposite side or opinion of what you really think or believe just for conversation. As you discuss and argue the point (that you don't believe) the others in the conversation will place that belief system on you. In their brain it will register as your position, as you're arguing for it, and they're arguing back. Never do this. Always make a point in "someone else's" place. You may say, "Well, someone else may see it as

...."Or, "Someone else might think that won't work because of ...." But don't ever take that fight on in your name. You don't believe it and they will remember it as your opinion.

Show genuine interest. This is something that isn't very common in our society today. Most people don't really listen to what the other person is saying. If you're hearing it, you're normally not truly interested in what they're saying and most likely thinking about something else. First, most people can tell when you don't care about what they're talking about. They know, and upon realizing it they'll cut their speech short, or change it up a bit to try to get your true interest. Second, if they're not able to tell by your body language, facial expressions, and intuition, then they will certainly be able to tell when they ask you a question about your opinion of what they just said. Nothing can flip a switch in someone like realizing that they just wasted all their time telling you something and you weren't even listening.

What typically occurs in our society is, people ask questions of others just to be nice, not really caring what the answer is. When you do this and then someone doesn't answer you, you really don't listen because you don't care.

This is evident with a simple experiment. Today as you walk around in public places, say hello to people you don't know. Many will ask you, "How ya' doin'?" "How are ya'?" or something to that effect. They'll do this while they're walking past you. They're not expecting an answer, and really don't care what your answer is. They aren't even going to slow down or look you in the face because they really don't care what you're going to say.

As someone asks you "How are you?" answer them as though you thought they really wanted to know. It will completely throw people off. We're used to people doing this every day, and don't think anything about it. If you want a real relationship with someone, then you must show genuine interest in what they are saying. If you really don't care, then don't ask the questions of them. The better thing to do is to realize that the subject does mean something to them, and it's important to them, so you should make it a point to listen and care as much as they do about it. This is repeated again a couple of paragraphs down.

People we run into every day have one thing in common. They're not our friends. They don't care about us or what is going on in our lives. If you want to stand out in someone's life, more than the typical stranger in society, you have to behave differently with them. Show genuine interest in what the other person is saying to you. What they are saying is important to them. If they care about it, then you should too.

The other part of this coin is for us to pay attention to our friends and see if they're listening to us. This is easy to do. I will simply throw an odd, or non- belonging phrase into the middle of a sentence and watch their reaction. If they don't notice precisely when it happens, then their mind is somewhere else. It is important to note that the people around us are actually listening to us and care about what we are saying. This will give you notice of your Alpha status, as well as the health of your relationship with that person.

You must demand that the people around you actually listen to you and show genuine interest in what you say. This will keep you both feeling good and keep the desire to continue the relationship. As you learned in the "You teach people how to treat you" chapter, this is another way of doing just that. Every time you feel that the other person isn't listening to you or doesn't care about what you are saying, throw in a curve ball. Turn your sentence into a question for them. Catch them off guard. They will feel embarrassed. After a few times of being caught off guard, they'll actually start to listen to what you're saying and start to participate more in your conversations, and that will lead to them actually being interested in what you're saying.

Always have an uncommon response to greetings from others. One thing that will really get a person's attention is when you answer their normal questions with unexpected answers. Actually, most people don't even expect you to answer their greetings at all. Things you hear all day long are things like: "How are you?" and,

"How you doing?"

If you stand near the entrance of a public place such as a retail store, you'll see this many times over. Watch how often this is done. Watch what people's responses are. When asked those common questions people will most often answer, "Good," or "I'm fine, thanks," or "Good, and you?" If you want to demonstrate to someone that you are different, then give them different stimulus. Give them a real, uncommon answer and watch their reaction.

This can be done with our friends as well. Friends will tend to greet each other the same way every time they see each other. Always use and respond with an uncommon greeting or reply to a greeting. Come up with something different. Use a phrase that no one else uses. This will show people that you are really talking to them and answering their question when they greet you. This does two things. First it defines you as an Alpha. You have your own mind and you assume that when someone asks you a question that they really care about your answer. Betas know that no one cares what they say. Second, this will make them feel good as you are the only person that day to truly respond to their inquisition. This fulfills both pillar requirements. This little change will make a big difference with a lot of people. Try it out.

Always walk in front. Always be the first one through the door. Always stand on the right. These are all things pertaining to our Alpha status. The person in front is the leader of the pack, literally. The first one through the door is the most respected, that's why your mother always told you to hold the door for ladies. It's internationally and instinctively recognized that the dominant or Alpha always stands on the right side. The right side means that if two people are standing or walking together, if you were both facing the same direction, the person in the power position would reach towards their left hand if you two were to shake hands. The beta would extend their right hand to the right.

Always be the first to end the conversation. The Alpha figure will end a conversation. His time is more precious and he has to go now. Whether it's on the phone or face-to-face, always be the first to end the conversation. Everyone has been through those conversations every week when you get to that point in the conversation that no one has anything else to say. You have that awkward moment. Don't let this happen. The moment you sense that you have no more to say to that person, let them finish their words and then immediately, after commentary if appropriate, let them know you have to go. That is a much better way to end a conversation.

When a conversation ends the standard way of nothing to say, it registers in the brain as awkward and not feeling good. To leave a great thought in their head every time, leave the conversation at a peak. It will leave them with a good feeling, and wanting to talk to you again. It leaves them hanging just a bit. It leaves them with a desire to do it again. They want you and it's a valid use of their time. This does not mean that we cut people off, or stop them from starting another sentence or story, it means that we are simply ending the conversation at a peak, when everyone is still having fun talking to one another. Don't let your conversations get boring.

After a conversation tell the person you're happy that you could help. Or, "I'm glad you got what you wanted." Or, "I'm glad you had a good time." Or, "I'm glad you caught me." Or whatever is appropriate. Don't thank them for coming or say, "I hope I helped," or, "Did you have a good time?"

A common mistake is for people to degrade themselves after talking with someone. This may seem like a nice thing to do, but it will program them how to treat you. The other person will walk away from each of your conversations with a sense of who's treat it really was. The goal is to be the Alpha and let the other person know that they're privileged to have talked to you. We don't say this as an egotistical thing, we just need this to maintain our value-added approach to this person. The way we end the conversation will leave them with an impression of "we helped them," and "that was good for them," or they will feel it was a waste of their time. You didn't add value to their life by conversing with them. We are simply trying to help them to realize that they got something out of their conversation with us. We, in return, should make a mental note that we enjoyed our time talking with them as well.

Favors. It's good to do favors for people that you like. You can do favors for people that don't like you as well, with the purpose being to develop a relationship with that person. Remember, all of these work under our first two pillars. They're also to be used with the other techniques in this book simultaneously. Use all or a combination of the techniques in this book together to get the results you desire. Often, only doing one thing will not work.

When you do a favor for someone else they owe you. Even the smallest things work, such as opening a door for them or greeting them. But it has to be done correctly. Simply helping people all the time and being a nice person will not get you the results you want. You will be seen as a pushover. You will program them to take advantage of you, not appreciate you.

The goal of doing a favor for someone is twofold. First, it makes you feel good about being of value and use to someone else. It also makes you feel good to help someone. Second, you need to make sure your actions are deliberate and produce a positive result with everything you do. A favor should program the other person to value you. To think about you. At this point you will be a positive experience in their life.

When you think about it, people will sum up a relationship they've had with another by weighing their experiences with them. Think about an ex-girlfriend or -boyfriend that you've had. When asked about that relationship, you will describe it as positive or negative depending on the number of good and bad experiences you had with that person. It's a sum total game. Most long-term relationships, even friendships, have ups and downs. Very few people experience a relationship where it was always good. But through this you have kept your best friend for years. Why? Because the good outweighs the bad. They are a value in your life as a whole. So it is with favors. Every time you do someone a favor you plant a good memory in their head. It's one more positive feeling that they register for you.

Every time we have a positive or negative interaction with someone, it registers in their brain and goes onto the scale. As long as the other person is taking it for granted that we're using our time and other resources to help them, then it's a good thing to do favors for other people. It shows our commitment to that friendship. It demonstrates that we are still plugged in and involved in that relationship. Women say this all the time. "My husband used to buy me flowers and write me nice letters, but not anymore." That is a valid point. The guy used to do things to demonstrate her value to him. But then eventually he took it for granted and stopped the favors that made her feel special.

It doesn't take major acts. It just takes an active thought of what you can do to really help someone and let them know that you still value them. If you have done a favor or something nice for someone, remind them of it. Ask them "How is that working out for you?" or "Did that fit ok?" This will remind them of the thing that you did for them and it will make them express their appreciation for what you have done. This is healthy, as it will make you both feel good about that good deed all over again. This is only to be done once, however.

Don't:

Don't always agree. Agreement is a tricky thing. How you agree with someone, or don't agree, will program a certain response from them. You may agree with someone when it benefits you. This is a way to show respect and maintain respect at the same time.

Agree with only a certain point or aspect of what someone says, reminding the other person that their belief or statement is only partially correct, and that they didn't think of this or that. This will program them for several things. They'll know that you're listening to them, acknowledging their beliefs and intelligence, and contributing to the conversation.

This will also help you to maintain their respect, as you don't simply go along with everything they say. You think for yourself, and you think differently from them. This tells them that you're an Alpha, and also that you contribute equally to the conversation or group. If you simply agree with everything everyone says, without challenging it intellectually or offering your own opinion on the matter, you will eventually program them that you're a follower. You will program them to be in charge and to be respected. This won't be healthy for your relationship. The other person will lose respect for you and not value you or your opinion as they did before. In return, you'll sense that and feel resentment towards that person for their feeling and treatment of you. Your relationship loses value and it may fade.

This isn't to say that you can't simply agree with your friend when they make a statement. You don't have to challenge everything. Where appropriate, and often, just add your point of view to the conversation and things will be much healthier. Relationships are about value. So keep adding value. Be very careful that you aren't bringing contention into the conversation. You don't want to create an argument by disagreeing all the time. You simply want to participate and add value to the relationship.

Compliments. These must be used carefully. This works hand in hand with "You teach people how to treat you." The rule is this: you compliment people for doing something you like such as "your shirt looks nice," if you do in fact like their shirt. If you do not like the shirt and tell them you do, you just programmed them to wear that stupid shirt around you again. You always compliment people for compliance with you, and for the behavior that you desire.

As we discussed before, people want to please others, and a relationship is the sum of all experiences together. Knowing this, if we tell them we don't like their shirt, then they'll want to please us and make us feel good around them by wearing a shirt that we approve of. When they do wear a shirt that we approve of, we mention that. They'll feel good that we like their shirt and approve of it, and it will register as a positive thought, tipping the weight in our relationship further to the good side. This will add to the total sum of positive thoughts and feelings towards us.

This works with any type of compliment. You can use this same programming when your friend brings a date that you don't care for. Let them know that you don't care for them. The night won't have a good feeling for them and it will be obvious. They'll not want to repeat that by bringing you two together again. Whatever the behavior, compliment the person for complying with your likes, and mention to them what you don't like.

This is a great form of programming that you can use every day. You may use this several times a day on the same person. You may say "I like your shoes." Then later you tell them, "I like how you said..... ." Again later you tell them "I didn't like how you talked to Steve." With every compliment of yours you reinforce and program them to behave as you would like.

Don't give explanations. It's hard to give an explanation without looking bad or wrong. The rule is, don't over explain yourself. There's a big difference between answering a person's question and defending yourself with an explanation. An extensive explanation looks like begging and is submissive behavior. At a certain point in your explanation it starts to register in the other person's brain as defensive speech. At this point your guilt is implied. The longer you explain yourself, the more guilty you look. You'll program the other person to go on the offensive and start to question and doubt you.

A short and direct explanation is the best way to answer a question. It may seem a bit brief and not what people are used to. But you will satisfy their question quickly and program them to not challenge you or pry for more details. What you must be able to discern is the difference between a question that requires an explanation or just an answer. We're asked questions all day long. From "What kind of bread do you want?" to "Can you pick me up from work?" These are honest questions that people use when they are simply looking for information from us. Other questions that people ask us are more derogatory in purpose. Their intent is to find guilt or question our motives. These are the questions that we will answer with direct short responses to.

Don't say, "I think." When making a point to someone you want to avoid stating, "I think." That makes it a matter of debate and begs for a rebuttal. Instead of using "I think," you should state the facts. This puts a whole different expectation on the comment. You state it as a fact if you believe it. An example could be, "I think that movie was great." This will immediately be challenged by another individual and your view will be beaten up. This is degrading in most situations. It starts a small frenzy of other's opinions bashing yours.

This may not seem like a big deal, but the way it registers in the brain is not charming for you. You tell your friends at lunch that, "I thought that movie was great." Everyone else will jump on that and tell you fifty reasons why you're wrong, what was wrong with the movie, and that it was in fact not great. This registers in their heads as a devaluation of your opinion. This occurs simply because you worded it wrong and set yourself up for rebuttal and not agreement.

Rather than use an "I think" statement you could say, "That movie was great because the actors were big names and the budget was huge." With that, the first thing people will do is agree with you. They see something specific that they can agree on. They may afterwards bring up something negative about the movie; however, this will register with them as reflected upon the movie and not you. The object will take the punishment and abuse, and you're not connected with it, all because you phrased it differently. Set yourself up for agreement and success when you speak. Don't make open-ended remarks that you'll have to defend. Look for ways to express yourself and your views in a way that people can agree with you.

Don't say, "Can you help me?" This is not a productive way to express your needs or desires. This puts you at the mercy of someone else and is a Beta label for you. The proper way to tell someone that you need assistance is to always say, "I need ...."

Again, it's all in how you frame it. By informing someone that you "need" this or that you imply that you're the Alpha and you expect help. It keeps you in a position of power, even though you need their assistance. It also registers in their brain as, "I get to help." You are an Alpha and people will offer assistance just to get brownie points with an Alpha. Everyone offers to help the boss, no one offers to help the mail guy in the office. It's all in how you present it.

This works with our two pillars. We are still being honest, and we are both benefiting. They will feel good about helping us accomplish our task, and we'll get the help we need. Always phrase your words and sentences from a position of respect. This does not mean that we aren't being humble. We aren't praising ourselves. We aren't putting ourselves out as better than someone else. We simply put ourselves out as someone to be respected. When your associates respect you, your relationships will be much healthier.

Don't answer an accusatory question. If someone asks you, "Why did you do this?", or "Why didn't you do that?" or "Are you ignoring me?" or anything accusatory, don't answer the question. You must respond with your own accusation or question to them. Direct the blame on them. Or project it on to someone else. But you can't make it look defensive for reasons we discussed earlier. Make it look as if they're mistaken or way out of line for questioning you, no matter how small or insignificant the question.

This is a part of "Teach people how to treat you." An example could be the very common "Are you ignoring me?" text, email, or voicemail that we've all received. In this case we wouldn't say, "No," plead for them to forgive us and explain to them why we haven't called them back. We must program them to behave more respectfully to us. A proper response would be something like, "I've had a very hard day today. I thought you would understand," or, "I've been trying to complete a project and assumed you would understand," or even, "I didn't realize you had an emergency. I've been terribly busy today, what's wrong?"

These responses put a whole new tone to the conversation. They now must fess up to being too demanding and explain why they behaved that way to you. Their wording of "are you ignoring me?" is derogatory, leading, and disrespectful. Neither one of us will feel good about this conversation if that tone continues. We must program them to realize that we'll respond on our own timeline, not theirs.

We have other important things going on and they must be patient. This will program them to value our conversations and their time talking to us. With this type of response from us they will be programmed to respect us and our time and their opportunity to share that with us.

The same works for us with our friends. We should never speak like that to them either. If they aren't responding and we don't know why, we should ask them if they're ok. We should not send a nasty message insinuating that they're purposefully and intentionally ignoring us. This also adheres to our two pillars. When asked any question, don't explain, just answer directly. Example: "Are you coming back to work?" "Yes." Don't explain where you're going or why you won't be back at a certain time. You don't answer to them.

To show dominance you always make people answer to or report to you. Instead of making a statement of disappointment ask a question making them accountable to you and answer for the discretionary act. For instance, don't make a statement saying, "This project is all messed up." Instead direct a question to the person, "Why is this all messed up?" This changes the dynamics and makes them accountable to you, and pushes the blame solely on them. This establishes your Alpha status and solidifies your dominance when they answer you, an outward sign that they accept you as Alpha. Otherwise they wouldn't defend themselves with an answer.

Never joke negatively about yourself. Likewise, don't ever joke about anything in a negative way that has to do with you or yours. For instance don't ever joke to someone that they "have to see you twice in one day." Instead always joke about a positive thing such as, "Hey, I'm glad you got to see me twice in one day." or, "You're lucky to see me twice in one day." The wording makes all the difference. Put a positive and cheerful emotion behind your words that will add one more good feeling to the relationship scale.

The typical way of joking negatively about yourself or your things or your people puts a negative spin on the occasion. This is a common mistake people make every day. It registers as a Beta trait, and the words weigh heavy in their brain as it was a self description. You gave them a one-sentence autobiography of yourself and it was negative. This will affect their behavior towards you. You'll feel better about yourself as well when your speech is positive and respectful of yourself. There are plenty of people in this world who will make jokes about you and tear you down without you doing it yourself.

Don't get casual with thanking others. Always say thank you when you really mean it and never use "thanks." One thing most people do wrong is to get too complacent with their praise to others. If you start saying thank you more to those around you, you will program them to keep doing good things for you. The people around us desire our praise. Everyone needs to feel needed. Don't short change yourself or those you're thanking with a half hearted "thanks." Always say thank you to show your appreciation. Everyone says "thanks," it's a standard response by most people. So you don't feel good when they say it because it's just an automated, haphazard response. Even with your family and close friends, always use thank you. It will register in their brain as another positive weight on your scale.

CHAPTER 22
Excuses

Making excuses for yourself rarely works. It always registers as BS. However, making excuses for others will win you points with the person you're defending as a way of forced teaming. It also programs others that you're on the same side as the person who screwed up and you'll get partial responsibility placed on you because you're defending them.

If you're looking to befriend someone, this would be a good way to make that happen. The person will see that you took a stand and defended them, even though they were seen as being in the wrong, and also that you had nothing to gain by doing it. This will win you some big points with the person you're defending. If you have the proper respect built with the others taking the opposite side, bending your stance and defending them will not erode that.

Whenever you see someone that is in a position of vulnerability it's a prime opportunity for you to develop a relationship by standing with them. This will occur when the person's views or actions are not seen as popular or mainstream, when a person is standing alone, or in the minority. People will feel overwhelmed, outnumbered, and out-of-control in these situations.

Your influence in this situation will score you big points in the mind of the person you're helping. At this point they're easily susceptible to programming as you've proven your loyalty and friendship in combination with their vulnerable mindset. This is also a form of loan sharking. You must be very careful at this point to stabilize your relationship on the two pillars. Because you've won points and loan sharked them, their vulnerability makes them highly susceptible to your programming.

As for making excuses for our own actions, we shouldn't do it. Everyone knows instinctively that no one is perfect. We all make mistakes occasionally and that's normal. The best thing to usually do is admit that a mistake was made and ask the person who noticed how it can be overcome. This puts the other person in a position of power and makes them feel better about our mistake because they're now able to add value to the situation. They feel needed and important and that they have something to offer. Deal with it like this and they'll have a good feeling instead of a conflicted feeling. You'll score a point from a screw-up because the other person will walk away feeling good about themselves and their ability to contribute.

However, if you try to defend yourself with an excuse it will rarely turn out as positive points in your favor. The other person is naturally suspicious of your story, will inquire with more questions, and it turns into an interrogation the more you defend yourself. At the end of it all, the other person most likely won't believe you anyway, and you'll score negative points with them.

Keep in mind that excuses are very different from explanations.

CHAPTER 23
Overcoming Prejudice

You will, on occasion, have to overcome a preconceived notion or prejudice against you. For instance, someone may not trust you or like you initially simply because you remind them of someone else that they don't like or trust. To overcome this you should talk about yourself and program them with who you are and that you are not the person you remind them of.

Some people will never like you simply because they are threatened by you. You have talents and abilities superior to theirs and they are uncomfortable with that. Your Alpha status will make you disliked by some as well. However most of the time this can be overcome.

When you've just met someone and they do not seem to like you it's due to a preconceived notion. This can be remedied quickly by referring to yourself by name and attributes. An example of this might be you telling a story as a third person and using your name repeatedly during the story. This will program them with your name and they will stop looking at you as though you were the other person that they don't like. You may look or sound or smell like someone that reminds them of something negative. However with the proper programming, they'll realize who you are and like you for being yourself, no longer seeing you as the other person.

CHAPTER 24
Social Physics

We all enjoy being around people that are like us. The physical partner to the agreement technique is called mirroring. This is a physical way to show your agreement and alignment with another person. In simple terms, it's copying their physical actions as though you are their reflection in a mirror. Sometimes we duplicate their actions and sometimes we just imitate or come close to copying their physical actions. As you observe people you'll notice that people enjoying the company of another will mirror each other. This is completely natural and instinctive human behavior. It's something humans do subconsciously when they feel a connection with another person.

You should pay close attention to social mirroring between yourself and the other person in your company. Mirroring will go a long way in solidifying that good feeling about you during a conversation. This doesn't mean that you act out their physical actions in real-time like a shadow. Most commonly seen are things such as crossing the arms or putting hands in pockets. When someone looks down at their feet and then moves their feet around their friend will normally mirror that action as well. This is a subconscious and subliminal message to the other person of friendship.

You should pay attention to this when you are engaged in conversation with people to make sure you're putting on a good feeling and scoring points for that interaction. You should also pay attention to the other person's actions to see if they mirror yours. If they aren't mirroring your actions, that's a subconscious sign to you that something is amiss.

A single negative indicator doesn't prove that something is wrong. But as we look and listen during our interactions with others we notice every detail and combine all of the data. They may be saying the right things to you but their actions and tone of voice betray their real feelings. We need to pay attention to all the details of our interaction to properly assess the stability and progress of our relationships. If you simply listen to their words you won't get the entire story and won't see that there may be trouble in your relationship. We need to know exactly how the other person is feeling about us so we know how to improve our relationship with them.

Some social mirroring involves full body movement. A person may turn in a different direction and take a step or two. A person may raise their arms and do a big stretch. Something you see all the time is one person will yawn and another person will yawn as well. This is all social mirroring. Most people don't even know they are doing it but subconsciously they will pick up on it when you do it to them.

Remember when you were in grade school and you told your mom that the kids were copying you? Your mother told you that they copy you because they like you.

Mom was right and people that want to subconsciously show their intention of friendship will partially copy your actions. Most often it will be the Alpha in the relationship that is being mirrored by the others in the group. By simple observance you can ascertain who is the Alpha of a group without being able to hear their conversation.

Social mirroring takes many forms. It can be any physical action that someone does similar to another's. One example might be that someone buys or downloads a song and then another person in the group gets that same song or album. Another common example is the way people greet. The Alpha in the relationship will decide what type of greeting will be used. It may be a simple hello, or maybe a handshake or fist bump, or it may be a hug. The Alpha will initiate the contact for the greeting and the other person will mirror that. You rarely see the other person refuse the greeting initiated by the Alpha and propose their own greeting.

Any physical manifestation of compliance or simulation is social mirroring.

CHAPTER 25
Solidifying Commitment

Once a person has begun the programming, a good way to solidify it is by making it public. This doesn't mean that you demean them or embarrass them in public, this means that after a person has committed an act in public, it will help to solidify that behavior.

Now remember that this can go both ways. If the person has been programmed to disrespect you, they'll most likely do it in public and it will not only become a habit, but they'll also feel pressured to repeat the behavior again in public because they have set a precedent for themselves in front of others. When the person has shown signs of acceptance to the programming and things are going well, this can be the time to have them express this in public, meaning in front of others; friends, family, etc. Open and public proclamations solidifies commitment. Most won't change opinion, stance, or behavior after they have committed to something publicly. This doesn't mean that they can't, and through programming they can change, but it's human nature to hold a position after you've done so publicly.

The best results come from the first public behavior being positive. You should be very aware of the behavior of the people you're programming while around others. If they treat you differently around other people, this must be addressed and corrected immediately, in front of other people.

Now, you must be careful when programming someone in public; don't let it appear to be ridicule, belittling, or public embarrassment. This can be a tough thing to do. What needs to happen to program this behavior out of them is to make it uncomfortable for them to do so. However, if you make it too embarrassing, then they'll openly and publicly resist and their behavior will get worse.

An example of this may be found in the following situation. You're at a dinner function for work. A coworker walks up to you at the party, with people standing all around and says, "If he (you) knew how to operate a computer, we would be getting home earlier every day." This is obviously a public display of disrespect to you in front of family and coworkers.

A proper programming response could be, "I'm the brains and the only computer guy on this project, wish I had help," or anything like this. This will generate a response from them that is defensive. They'll now try to convince the crowd that they do contribute at work. The focus just went to them. Next time, he'll probably not make another comment like that to you. His intention was to be funny and make himself look good by making a derogatory statement about you. However, by your response, it turned into an embarrassing attempt to justify himself. It was all done non-aggressively, and not initiated by you. It was done immediately and in public to let them know that you won't be the butt of a joke in front of others.

The same works for submissive or respectful public displays. Often a good way to effect this is to initiate it. Be the first person to say something positive about them in the company of others. If the programming has progressed to a good level, they'll accept it graciously and return the compliment. This is the response that we're looking for. If, however, the person gets a big head over your public statement about them and their ego starts to get carried away, you'll know that more programming is necessary before you attempt it again in public.

The point here is to take notice of their behavior and treatment of you in front of others. Pay attention to what and how they behave with all statements involving you. This is also reciprocated by you. You show the others around you that you respect them and they'll notice that. That will make them want to be around you and your friends. They'll start to mirror and emulate your friends and the way they treat you as well. They'll feel good and behave properly around your friends because they see that your friends treat you with respect, and they'll follow suit.

Another concept that goes along with this is Participation. Participation is key. Get them involved and interactive and they'll be committed. This is a tactic commonly used by marketing and sales firms. They'll quickly get you plugged into a group and get you excited about the project and get you involved immediately. The more time and resources someone puts into anything the more committed they'll be. "It's too late to turn back now I have too much invested," and, "Everyone has seen me doing this so I can't admit I was wrong and change now," are attitudes that will help drive them forward. So get them plugged into your life and your goals, and then show them how your life and goals align with theirs. Once they actually start participating by behaving differently, especially around others, they'll commit to the change and make it a habit. They'll now be participating and will instinctively want to behave the way you do.

Another concept to keep in mind is that you learn to love the things you suffer for. Public scrutiny is suffering. This all plays into the part of your programming wherein you solidify their behavior by them doing it in front of others. Suffering is a price paid for something.

Ask any Special Operations guy, PhD, or Olympic athlete; they've all suffered to get where they are. Once you have paid the price, you hold on to your accomplishment. It turns to a love and a passion, and part of who you are. It becomes part of your identity. Behavior is no different. Once the person has behaved properly in public, they've paid a price (suffered) publicly and won't want to reverse that. Because you will praise and reward them, as well as the people around you, for their behavior, they will desire to continue that same behavior. Make no mistake, public scrutiny is suffering, and once they have behaved properly and passed public scrutiny, they'll be programmed to continue the correct behavior, as long as they're rewarded for it.

SECTION 5: FORMAT AND REINSTALL

This is the programming that you will need to alter behavior in an existing relationship. The brain code in this section will help you transform your current relationship into something enjoyable.

CHAPTER 26
Call to Action

Most people cannot or will not read between the lines when it comes to what they need to do. You need to request action in clear and respectful terms. During the programming stage it's important that you are clear on what is expected from them.

This sort of thing often causes problems as people are unclear as to what they desire and then become upset when the other person doesn't fulfill their desires. A call to action with clear direction must follow all of the other principles in this book.

It's difficult for people to get others to do what they want them to without the added burden of trying to guess exactly what it is that you desire from them. Again, you can't make this sound disrespectful to them or others around them and you can't make it sound as if you're giving them an order. You're following the programming rules and are paying attention to the details and description that you're giving them.

I'm sure you've experienced a situation where someone has asked you to do something for them and you tried to fulfill their wish and ended up disappointing them. You had the earnest desire to fulfill their request and you felt good about what you did; however, it ended with both of you feeling unhappy.

This happens to us all the time. This is all because the details and description are not given completely. This one simple thing is what will turn ordinary tasks and arguments into reliable and dependable feelings in a friendship. If you're not absolutely clear about what you want, the programming won't take effect. You can't correct an action that they did when they were actually trying to fulfill your request. You also can't reward someone for the wrong action or behavior, even though it's due to your lack of clarity in giving instructions.

You must have the proper respect for their knowledge, education, resources, and experience in mind when making your request. This means that you can't explain things to them like you would to a child if they aren't a child. You can't give common sense details to them if they're able to reason that out on their own. This will be taken as disrespect, and an outward show that you think they are stupid. This will be the opposite of productive in the programming process.

Know what details they will need to fulfill your request and then leave the rest to their own intelligence. This must all be adjusted on an individual basis. The mental capacity of everyone is different. Some people are not good at putting certain disciplines together, they will need more specific direction in those cases.

An example of this may be a request to help you assemble a piece of hardware. Some people aren't good at this kind of a thing. Without insulting their intelligence and making them feel dumb, you'll need to give them more specific direction as to how to perform the task. However, give the minimum amount of details needed by that person to get the job done adequately. Whatever action it is that you need from them, you need to make it clear to them that you're asking them for it.

Do not hint or insinuate that you need something done. They may not take the hint and will disappoint you both. Be clear on the fact that you are requesting something from them and explain how you want it done. If you don't ask them, they may not even think about doing it. By simply asking them in clear terms, you may just get what you want.

CHAPTER 27
Demand Respect of Your Time

Everyone is busy. This is a very busy age that we live in. No one has extra time that hasn't been planned out. One common way that people get taken advantage of is by demands of your time. People seldom ask for things that don't involve your time. It seems the more you do for some people, the more they ask you to do. "It's because you're reliable." Or, "It's because you're a great friend."

Often this isn't the case. It's usually a matter of respect and pecking order. You're often asked to give of your time because your time seems worth less than someone else's time. When you always say yes, not because you're a "nice person" or you're a genuinely good friend in their view, it's often seen as you are the person that has nothing more important to do while everyone else around you does. It's all about perception. You're asked over and over again to give your time because they know others are too busy. When you say yes, to most people it registers in the brain as you have nothing better to do. This isn't always the case, but often it is. If not, why don't they keep asking the person who said no the first three times they asked them? If this weren't the case, other people would be asked before you. But they always ask you first because you are the "least busy" and the highest probability of a yes in their mind.

Most people fall into this trap innocently, and then don't know how they got there or how to get it to stop. Most of us are willing to help when we are genuinely needed. So the first time you say yes, you're now labeled as "the not busy person" who has nothing important to do. You're not seen as a saint or otherwise kind, caring person.

You'll be seen in their mind as the person whose time is less important than theirs and the others around them.

It's easy to try to be nice and help someone and get all caught up in this trap of slave labor and ungrateful service to others. The problem works both ways on this issue however. You're an obvious victim because you're used and abused and not even recognized for your sacrifice of helping them. They also lose in this because you will see them as a user, not as a friend. This will change your relationship. You will both lose out.

The proper response is to always be busy. Because you're truly busy like everyone else, this isn't hard. You must simply let that person know how busy you are and that it will be a burden to you to change things to make yourself available for them. Instead of just saying "yes", you should let that person know that you already have plans. Don't dramatize it, simply let them know that you are busy and have other important things to do.

Don't ever tell someone "no problem." It is a problem. You do have things to do, and you will have to make arrangements and sacrifices to accommodate their wishes of taking your time. Let them know that you desire to help them, but you have to make arrangements with your schedule to make time for them. That shows them you are as busy as everyone else, and it shows them that it really is a sacrifice, and not a privilege, to help them out. You show them that your helping them is a big deal, because you really don't have the time to do it. So when you do come through for them and help, it's greatly appreciated and not brushed off as "no big deal."

The other side to your time is how others delay on your demands. All of us have been left waiting by others. Everyone has experienced that feeling of anxiety when the other person didn't make the deadline. This may have been a ride to pick you up, or a co-worker not getting his part done. By always letting them know that you're busy, they'll know they can't be late and delay on help or requests from you.

This will make a big difference not only in your performance, but also in your relationship with that person. They will be forced to be reliable and prompt when dealing with you. If the person thinks that your time is not important, then they will constantly be late. They believe their time is more important than your time. You can wait on them. This falls directly in line with Chapter 7: You Teach People How to Treat You.

You must constantly let people know that you already have plans and that you're always busy whenever someone asks for your time. This doesn't mean that we don't help people, it simply means that we're making them aware that our time is valuable. Promise that person that you'll try to rearrange your schedule to see if you can help them, but don't promise them you'll do it right away.

This will reprogram their behavior. It will be a shock to them the first time you tell them "you don't know" if you're available to help them. They'll usually try to make a joke at your expense, something to the effect of "what are you doing?" or "got a hot date?" After you simply state the fact that you already have plans, and you might be able to rearrange your schedule to help them, their attitude will change.

The best way to break the habit of people taking advantage of your time is by simply telling them no. Tell them you have something important to do and can't help them. The next time they ask you to do something, their attitude will be different. They won't automatically assume that you'll be at their beck and call from that time forward.

A typical response to this is that some people will try to shame you into helping them by making you feel guilty. They may even ignore you for a while and ask others for help in front of you. This is an attempt to make you think their time is worth more than yours. They want you to desire their attention. They want to punish you for saying no to them. Many will try different tactics to get you to feel bad about saying no to them. However, after a while, most will come around and ask you again. This time they will be more respectful of your time and resources.

Again, this works in tandem with our two pillars. First, we are being honest about being busy. We are all busy and cannot just jump up and go somewhere for a person any time they desire. Second, this is mutually beneficial as we both respect each other and work better together like this. We'll feel much better about helping them and donating time when we know we aren't taken for granted. They too will benefit as we'll actually treat them better because we know that they now value us and our time. They'll benefit by us being dependable and reliable because we're their friend. Friendship and respect will be gained by both sides where there was none before.

CHAPTER 28
Demand a Thank You

When you've done something for someone, no matter how small, you should always get a thank you. If the person doesn't immediately offer a thank you, give them a friendly nudge by saying, "You're welcome." This will instinctively make them thank you. Once they've verbalized it, they will recognize what you've done for them mentally. It will now be a conscious thought of you doing them a favor. They just made a mental note of it. Also, this is a form of loan sharking. As we discussed before, by you bringing it to the forefront of their attention they recognize that we've done something for them, something that we didn't have to do. By them thanking you, they now accept that you did them a favor and they owe you.

Our intention here is not to get "paid back" with another favor from them. Our intended consequence here is to force that person to acknowledge the good deed we did and to take note of it. This is a way for us to constantly reinforce that we're a value to them.

A good relationship needs constant attention, consistent reinforcement of its worth. A continual reminder of our contribution is healthy for both parties. We'll feel good that we're acknowledged and recognized for the things we do, and they'll feel good because they know we're plugged in and committed. They know that we still care.

This will also strengthen respect. As long as you demand a thank you from them, they'll have to continue showing you respect. The words, "Thank you," show respect. In the brain, it registers as respect. We know this because it's always difficult to thank someone that you don't like or are mad at. It's not hard to say it because they don't deserve it for their action, it's hard to tell them because we are not happy with them right now.

For this reason alone, it's good to get a thank you. It's one of the simplest ways for you to get respect from someone who doesn't like you or respect you. Forcing them to say thank you will start programming them to treat you differently. A thank you gives worth and value to someone. It's something that is recognized by everyone around that hears them say it to you. A thank you goes a long way.

CHAPTER 29
Extra Credit

If you want to build a relationship with someone, or make an existing relationship better, you can tell them thank you even though you've done something for them or they haven't done anything for your. This obviously must be done with good timing and in the right context. You can't simply blurt out the words thank you randomly as it will mean nothing. On occasion and near the end of a conversation with someone find a way to say thank you for something no matter how small it was.

Thank you is an expression of appreciation and it will score positive points every time you use it. These words can obviously be overused and program a person for the wrong behavior. However, when used appropriately and sparingly, it will build a good feeling in them about you. It lets the other person know that you appreciate the little things about them. You not only recognize and appreciate the big things they do, but you also cherish all of the little things that make them unique.

This is not something that you will do all the time, nor is this something that you will demand a response or reply to. This is the extra credit question on a test. This is that little bonus point you get after a positive score conversation or interaction.

Do not overuse this. This is one of those things that will score you some extra positive points when used on occasion. "Thank you," is also a form of loan sharking because you've done something nice, i.e. thank them, and also because you gave them a good feeling they will now desire to reciprocate. Saying thank you to someone after you've done something for them can also score big bonus points. It registers that you truly desire to be with them

and serve them as a loyal friend. It's a demonstration of your commitment to the friendship and your desire to make the other person happy.

CHAPTER 30
Changing the Status Quo

Another absolutely critical part of manipulating someone's behavior is to change their status. Behavior won't be altered if the status isn't altered. The definition of insanity is to repeat the same process over and over again expecting different results. To change behavior you have to change the pattern, and this means you must change the stimulus.

One of the most effective ways to change someone's actions is to change the consequences. The other person must believe that real and/or unfavorable consequences exist. You must be convincing. If the person doesn't believe that these consequences are real (meaning you will follow through), that person's behavior won't change. The other side of the motivation is to offer a positive consequence for an appropriate action. It may work either way. You may find that a reward works better than a punishment with many people.

For instance, let's take a coworker. Let's say this person only talks to you when they must for work related activities. They don't greet you in the morning or talk to you at lunch. This person only talks to you when they must ask you about something for work or to give you a task for work. To change the status quo in this situation, you must address the issue. The best option is to address it directly.

You might wait until this person comes to you for a work related task and asks you to do something. At this time, state the fact that they only talk to you formally for work. If the person gets embarrassed, as most people will, then they'll apologize and start a conversation. That same day they'll start saying hello to you and also make small talk with you. That will now be the normal status if you keep it going, and stay friendly with that person.

If that person has a different reaction, say more confrontational, they may reply with a snotty remark such as, "We're not friends," or something similar. In this case make it known to them that their choice to not be friends means that you have no personal commitment to helping them at work. Tell them that you'll do your job, but won't go out of your way in any form that will benefit them at work. Let them know not to expect any favors or extra effort in the work you do that benefits them. This will make it clear to them that there are immediate and effective repercussions for not being friendly to you.

Here is another example. Let's say you have a close friend, and this friend has a new girlfriend. This new girl doesn't get along with you. For whatever reason she doesn't treat you well. Every time the three of you are together she either ignores you or treats you badly.

One way you might change her behavior is to make it clear to her that pleasant experiences will come if she is nice to you. Take the opportunity to plant the idea in her head the next time she says something nasty to you. Tell her that if she would be a little bit nicer to you that you could make sure they get more private time together. Or, let her know that if she is nicer to you that you will support your friend dating her and encourage your friend to continue the relationship. This can have immediate and lasting results. The girlfriend must now acknowledge that you do have some power and control over her comfort in this relationship, and that by being nice to you, she will benefit.

You've just seen an example of the two different ways to manipulate someone's behavior with consequences. One is positive, and one is negative. It normally won't hurt to try the positive avenue first. If that doesn't work, then you can switch tactics to the direct, and more negative consequential approach.

All of this has to do with changing their status. Sometimes we'll change their status (or standing) with us, and sometimes we'll affect their status with others. Both of these were seen in the two examples above. In the first example, we changed their status from the dominant person in the "relationship" at work, to being an equal or subservient to us because we can affect their life negatively. In the second example we changed their status from being the dominant friend of our friend, to being in second place behind us.

Many people will be happy having a dominant or higher status, and they act like it. We all know these kind of people. They treat people like garbage because they can, simply based on their status. So this tells us that by changing their status, or at least threatening to change their status and having the ability to follow through, we can change their behavior.

Some people may be very difficult to work with. They may be very nasty all the time. But when they realize that you can change their status, for better or worse, most will conform to your wishes of acceptable behavior. The key is to find the one thing that can change their status.

Some people treat everyone terribly because they can. But when you find that one thing that can change their status, you'll change their behavior. An example might be the office jerk. This guy walks around all day being rude and disrespectful to everyone. Everyone hates him and he knows it. He actually kind of likes it because it gives him a feeling of power.

To this kind of person, changing his status with the group he treats badly is of no consequence or importance to him. It won't affect him. Most people desire to be liked, but these kinds of people trade that feeling of friendship for a feeling of power. So telling him, "Everyone here hates you," or, "If you don't start being nice to people, everyone here will hate you," won't work on this guy. He is happy with the power he feels more than the unpleasant feelings he feels with his coworkers.

In this case, you must change his status with someone he does have to worry about. You can make it known to him that there will be negative consequences for him with his boss if he continues his normal treatment of coworkers. You may get with all of the others that are mistreated and go to his boss all as one. You may make it known to him that he needs you, and that if you didn't do your best his project performance would suffer, and hence his boss wouldn't be happy with any of the work coming from his department. Make it known to him that if you're not happy at work, that your performance might slip or that you can't be expected to continue to put in the extra effort every day that makes him and his projects look good to his boss.

The bottom line here is that everyone has someone that they value their relationship with and whose opinion they value. When you're mistreated, make it known to that person that you can change their status with that person. In many cases we ourselves are that someone. We're the person that they want to be liked by. In some cases we're not, but we can always find a way to change a person's status with someone they do care about, for better or worse. And that is a game changer.

CHAPTER 31
Habits

For the most part people treat you the way they do because it has become a habit. In the beginning of your relationship, or somewhere along the way, you programmed them to treat you exactly as they do. It's human nature to push things to the limits when dealing with others to see how far we can tip the scales to our benefit. This is something you'll find yourself doing as well, so you must be conscious of this as to not take advantage of those around you.

At times everyone gets in a position of mental weakness or vulnerability and it's at that time that human nature tells us to take charge and manipulate others.

Instinctively and subconsciously you may attempt to push them into a position that gives you more power. When you find someone in that position remember to put everything in context and base your actions upon our two pillars and then everything will work out for a benefit to both of you.

Understanding now how you have most likely done this to someone else, we can see how easy it is for people to begin disrespectful behavior towards us. Most of the time good people will not consciously think about treating you badly. This happens because you allowed it to happen in the past and it has become a habit. They're doing it subconsciously. Because they aren't consciously planning to treat you badly they can be easily programmed to discontinue that behavior. When done properly Behavioral Programming will be a very smooth and natural transition into more appropriate behavior.

A person who argues with you about a statement of programming that you made to them is making a conscious decisions about what they say to you and how they treat you. When someone argues with you or immediately picks up on your programming, know that their behavior is intentional and their conscious desire is to treat you exactly the way that they are. This is an obvious indication that this person is really not your friend and doesn't have your best intentions at heart.

Brute force brain hacking is the way to solidify the programming and turn it into a habit. Habits are formed by behaviors repeated over and over again. Behavioral Programming programs a different behavior and turns it into a subconscious habit.

For most people habits are quite hard to break. Most people desire structure and repetition in their lives. Consistency is a way of life for most people. This means that if you have known a person for any length of time and they treat you inappropriately it's because you've reinforced that habit with repetition and consistency.

The same is with our strategy of brute force brain hacking; it involves repetition and consistency on our part as we bombard their brain with all of the programming techniques. This will develop new behavioral habits and will program them for long-term acceptable behavior.

So as you're reviewing your relationships with your friends and colleagues and how they treat you, you must realize that you've programmed them to treat you as they do. It's difficult to think of a time that is inappropriate to start Behavioral Programming.

With every interaction you're either endorsing a person's behavior or programming them to change it. The longer you endorse their habits of behavior the longer it can take them to be fully programmed to a new behavior.

The best time to start your programming is with your very next interaction. The easiest way to start is normally via digital communication such as text or email.

CHAPTER 32
Lying

If people lie to you it's because you make them uncomfortable with your reaction to the truth. Remember, you teach people how to treat you. You have taught them two things; first, you taught them that you'll make them feel worse about telling you the truth. Second you taught them that you'll accept their lies. These actually are two parts of the same thing and can be remedied quite easily.

First, examine how you react to that person when they give you a true but inappropriate excuse why something wasn't right. Do you get harsh? Do you accuse them and make it out to be a personal and deliberate insult to you? Do you "discipline" them with words or deeds or possibly ignore them for a while? Do you make a big deal out of their behavior?

When you look at all of these things the bottom line comes down to how you make them feel. At the end of your interaction they feel bad. Therefore they'll start to lie to you because they feel better after having done so rather than feel your wrath. This isn't to say that they don't bear responsibility for their deceit, it simply means that you didn't address the actual action (being late for example) with programming, and you programmed them to lie to you rather than change their behavior.

If people lie to you in the very beginning of your relationship it has most likely become a habit for that person as other people have programmed them to do so. However you'll find that most people lie to others on a case-by-case basis. They have been programmed by each person as to who they will lie to and who they will be brutally honest with no matter how embarrassing the facts may be.

Some people just don't care, their free life attitude makes whatever you say acceptable and will not "judge you." This will program you to open up to them and be honest with them always. However, this attitude is not a real value add to your relationship. Everyone needs people in their lives that will give them prudent and honest advice. This "judgment" isn't about you, it's a reply to the situation.

Your real friends that care about you will be honest, and not always agree with you and your actions. They'll challenge your ideas and behaviors that they feel aren't beneficial to you. This seems to become a major hang-up for some people.

Some people don't want to hear the truth, they simply want to hear support. These people tend to be less honest themselves, not wanting to "butt in" to your private decisions. But the reason that you open your personal life and decisions up to those trusted few is to get a detached and alternate view to double check your decisions.

This all goes along with people wanting to help others and avoiding unpleasantness. They will lie to you to make themselves feel better, and they will also lie to you to make you feel better. How many times have you "beaten around the bush" or taken the long, soft way around breaking the news to a friend or family member? Most likely, most every time you spoke to them about something controversial. This is also a learned or programmed behavior. You've been programmed to soften the blow when delivering bad news or disagreement by the way they responded the last time you tried that.

You've been programmed by each individual as well. You'll react the way they have programmed you to by their reactions. As you think about the different people in your life, you can readily recall who you speak openly to and who you hold back details from. Usually this is because "you don't want to hear it." That is a standard answer when you confide details with someone and they ask, "Did you tell so-and-so yet?" You normally answer with, "No, I don't want to hear it," or some close variation.

This in itself explains the motivation for people to not be open and honest with each other. This is the reason that you do it, and everyone else does it as well. You don't want to hear it even though you know what they will say

127

is probably correct.

Or sometimes you don't want to hear it from certain people because you don't want to hear their unhelpful thoughts on the subject. Some people will just give you dumb answers all the time and not be able to see your point of view or common sense at all.

Whatever the case, all of these people have programmed you how to converse with them individually. One by one they've programmed you to be open with them or to conceal all or part of the situation. You've done the same with all of the people in your life. You have programmed them by your behavior (your responses) to be truthful to you or not to be.

To remedy this, think of the person or people in your life that you're very open with and you'll realize how they behave when you tell them things. The secret to programming people to be truthful with you all the time is to imitate what you like from those you are most open with. React the same way to your friends and they'll in turn find that they're comfortable being truthful with you.

CHAPTER 33
Choices

Choices should not be given to people in the beginning stages of programming. Choices put people in a position of power and authority. Since we already have a behavioral problem with respect and submission, giving them choices will not benefit us at this stage. Choices are something that will come later and will be part of the rewards and reinforcement program.

In the beginning stages of programming you should give people only specific direction, not choices. For instance, you have a desire to meet up with this person. They are constantly standing you up, or are consistently very late. You would simply tell them where to meet you and at what time. Say meet me at our Italian restaurant at six on Wednesday. The wrong thing to do would be to ask them if they want to meet you at that time or place. What would also be wrong is to ask them to pick the time or place.

In the early stages of programming they shouldn't be given choices but should simply comply with your requests if possible. That being said, you must be sure that your requests are appropriate and feasible for the other person. Often times it is truly inconvenient or inappropriate for the person to comply with the request and people interpret that as resistance. If your request is reasonable and there is no prudent explanation as to why they cannot comply with your request, then that is resistance.

The reason behind this technique of programming is to establish respect for you and your desires and time from the other person. This is not in any way done to demoralize or control the other person, this is strictly done as a way to program respect for you into the other person the same as you show them. This can be done face-to-face or via digital media.

One thing that you must remember is how you frame the statement. Your tone of voice, body language, and presence of others will have a large factor in their determination of whether to comply with your request or not. You can easily thwart your own request by using the wrong tone or body language. You must avoid your statement being taken as an order. It must come off respectful, or the natural tendency will be for people to decline.

You must also remember that others may be present during your request, so it must come off looking respectful in front of them. If the other people around take your statement as a sign of disrespect, the person will decline your request simply to avoid the label of "pushover" from the others. Other people's opinions can have a great influence on a person's behavior. Don't make requests look like an ultimatum.

Remember, every interaction with the person must be a positive one.

Ultimatums will always register in the brain as coercion. Make the request happy and fun and firm. It's firm because you've already organized all the details. Who, what, when, where, and how. It's all ready to go, all they have to do is show up and have a good time.

`Further into their programming you can start to offer choices. As you see their attitude change, and you're both happier with your interactions, at this point you can change it up a bit and add in choices for them. The choices should be offered on the specifics, not the dos and don'ts.

For instance, you can now offer the person a choice of what time or where to meet you. This demonstrates equal respect for both of you. You are requesting an activity (your get-together), and they choose the details that work for them. You're both making the decision and agreeing on it. You're both respecting the other person, this is a win-win situation.

What you don't want to do is to completely reverse the roles by asking them if they want to meet up with you, what time they want to meet, and where they want to meet. This is not to say that you never do this, this is kept in mind for all the people that you are still programming and working to strengthen your relationship with. Once a relationship is fully matured and all parties are happy, then this won't matter. However, this is really a big deal when programming people that don't treat you properly.

CHAPTER 34
Direction Change

Sometimes during a conversation things will start to go wrong. Typically the conversation won't start out negative or combative. Many times however, at some point in the conversation, one side will become irritated by their interpretation of a statement. Too often conversations start out between people as normal or joking and at some point it turns to someone being offended. Other times you'll be trying to make a point and somehow things get pushed off course or otherwise deviate from the point you were trying to make. If, for whatever reason, the conversation takes a turn for the worse, and things are not going as planned, you can simply distract the other person with a question.

If you ask someone a question it will distract them from the current conversation or line of thought. If a conversation is not going your way, you simply ask them a question to get them off that topic. The more strange or off- topic the question is, the harder it will be for them to come back to the current topic or remember their talking points. These results increase the longer you talk off topic.

This is a great way to handle a situation that is getting uncomfortable or out of control. When it's a normal conversation and it turns into a dispute, one that will possibly leave a negative score, then it's time to abruptly changed directions and salvage your points for this particular conversation. This is perfectly in line with our two pillars as you're not being deceitful, you're simply changing topics to a more pleasant conversation. The other pillar is also satisfied because everyone involved will benefit from a more comfortable and pleasant conversation.

This must all be done tactfully and correctly. If you ask a question that is completely outside the scope of anything currently being discussed it will be dismissed as they recognize the attempt to change the topic. At this point things are most likely getting heated and people have things they want to say to prove their point. You must be very careful asking a question that is deviating as much as possible from the current topic but that can be accepted as a general topic discussion relating to the conversation.

Give the other person a brief time to answer and discuss the question that you just proposed and then change the subject a few more degrees off of the original by asking another question. By the second question things should be completely off-topic and all parties should be relaxed and rationally discussing the new topic that you have introduced.

Remember, once things get heated and disagreeable statements are made, the entire experience will register as a negative score. The sooner that you can change the topic, the easier the transition and the likelihood of a positive outcome and score. You must put aside your ego immediately when things start to go sideways. No matter how correct you are, or how much you believe that you can prove your point, you're probably not going to win this one. You may prove your point, but you'll come out with a pretty big negative score. That's not a win.

Scoring points with them will benefit both of you better than you proving this single point right here and now. You'll keep the respect and status that you've gained and your power to influence the other person will still be intact.

CHAPTER 35
Sympathy

When you're trying to generate a specific response from an individual, you can invoke the sympathy tactic. Let's say you want someone to do something for you, but you know that they "can't" or at least shouldn't. It's against the rules. Use sympathy to get them to do you a favor and take a risk for you. In other words, use sympathy to tip the scales in favor of doing something that they otherwise would not do. They will know that they have nothing to gain from doing this thing. They can only lose by doing it. That's the feeling that you have to change.

Let's say that I want to get my car repaired quickly. Who doesn't, right?

Everyone else waiting for the shop to fix their car would like theirs put first also. The policy of the shop clearly states that they work on a "first come, first served" basis. I would engage the man behind the counter in a conversation directed at my need for fast repair. He hears this every single day, and would normally brush me off and blame it on the policy, "I would help you if I could, but there's nothing I can do."

We've all heard this response before. Everyone has. Most of us have tried begging and bribing and everything in between to get them to budge. I would start by building rapport with the mechanic. I would find out how his day is going, and what makes him tick. I'd do this very quickly, to not let him get bored, or nervous that he is spending too much time with me. I would ask very simple, direct questions as though I really care about his problems. Then I would find the one piece that also fits me.

For example, I might say, "You guys look really busy today." He would most likely reply, "Yes, very." Of course he is, that's why my car won't be out of here for three weeks. So I then tell him that I understand how hard it must be, how hard the work must be, and how he must have tight timelines for getting the work done.

Then he would say, "Yes, we have to keep on it and get the cars done quickly so we can get on to the next one," or something to this effect. I would then ask if his boss gets upset if things take longer than expected, even if it wasn't his fault. He would tell me yes, and go into some detail about his boss doesn't understand and that it's not really his fault.

Now I will tell him that I too, have a boss like that, or a wife, or whatever person closely mimics his overseer. I would say that I also must meet my timeline or I will suffer as he does. He'll now start to feel sympathy for me as he completely understands and relates to my problem as his own.

Now we're really cooking. After this, he'll most likely come up with some sort of idea about how he can get my car done faster, because he now feels my pain. He now has sympathy for me because he experiences the same thing, and he knows he is the cause of that pain on me. He just got done telling me how terrible it was that he was held accountable for things beyond his control. Now he doesn't want to tell me that he's going to do the same to me. It's not right that his boss does it to him, so he won't do it to me.

What we've changed here is that he now has something to gain and lose. He gains a good feeling by helping me avoid the injustice of my boss, for punishing me for something beyond my control. He loses the feeling of not being in control of his life.

He can't control his boss, but he can help me control mine. It's pretty much the same thing for him. Because I have grouped us together, and our bosses together, he is actually, in his mind, helping us both.

Sympathy works two ways. You must show sympathy to get it. Most of the situations you find yourself in will require you to show the other person sympathy first. The next step is for you to cause the other person to have sympathy on you, and then use that sympathy to change their behavior to something more favorable for both of you.

How do our two pillars stand up here? First, our pillar of honesty is in play.

We're not going to lie to this guy about our situation. We're going to be truthful about our circumstances, and that will show. We're going to be sincere in our questions to him as well. He can tell if you actually care how his day is going, and he can also tell if you relate to his predicament and show real concern for his troubles.

Our second pillar is also at work. We both come out of this feeling better. We obviously feel good about getting our car repaired faster than normal, and this gentleman feels better because he got to help someone in need. It also gives him back a bit of control in his life. Most of us have the majority of our daily activities dictated by someone else. This man has a boss who tells him what to do all day long. In this case, the man gets to make a decision and that gives him a good feeling about himself and it gives him a little control over his life.

CHAPTER 36
Order of Words

You should always be very deliberate in the words you choose. Part of that is the order that you place words. Most people don't pay any attention to the order of their words, they simply say what they're thinking and the words come out randomly without any thought to what the difference will be in the other person's interpretation.

You must be very selective of the order that you present your information, as to program another person with just the right thing.

An example of this would be the all too common, "No, thank you." This is often an answer to someone's question to you. The problem is that it registers incorrectly in their brains. Your intention is to politely tell that person no. But you start the phrase with a negative, and that is what will register the strongest in that person's head. The best way to answer a question negatively is to put the positive "thank you" first. "Thank you, no," is the correct way to express a negative answer.

One thing about this is that, "No, thank you," is so commonplace that the person will probably not get a feeling of anything. It's a standard response that people are used to hearing daily. As we discussed in another chapter, to program people to respect you and listen to you, you must speak uncommonly. By saying, "Thank you, no," we express our gratitude first, and that is what will register with them. It's also a much less used response that they don't hear all the time. This will give them a good feeling, even though we just told them no.

Think about this; a person is at a party, or workplace, and they've asked people "Would you like a cookie?" all night long. Every person present has told her, "No, thank you," all night long. Your unique response will register with them. By simply being different, they know that you actually listened to them, and thought about your answer to engage them. That is unique because no one else did it.

You don't want to be seen like everyone else. If you're seen the same as everyone else around you, you'll be treated just like everyone else. You want to be treated special. You want to be respected and seen as having value to them above others. You can't accomplish this by being just like everyone else. You must be unique. A common theme throughout this book is being very careful of your word selection. This whole book is about the words you use. So by using your words differently than others, you will be seen differently than others.

You use words effectively and deliberately to program others to think and feel as you would like them to. Many people just say what's on their minds. The new theme out is "be tolerant and accepting." This whole philosophy is bogus. You're the most boring and unintelligent person in society if you don't have your own views, opinions, feelings, or beliefs about anything someone else says or does. There really isn't much to you at all at that point.

Whether people admit it or not, they truly do have feelings and thoughts and beliefs on the opinions or views you express. Knowing this you need to be deliberate about what you say and how you say it so you always convey your true intentions, and convey them in a way that gives the other person a reason to respect you.

You must speak in a way that makes others feel good about you, even if they disagree. You know that everyone has thoughts, ideas, feelings, and beliefs on just about any subject you may bring up and talk about. So use your knowledge of language and brain registration of words to give people what they want by the way you verbally express your thoughts. Use your speech to program them to react exactly the way you expect them to act.

CHAPTER 37
Compromise

Do not compromise when someone rejects or disappoints you. I recently had a friend who expected and planned to meet with a girl. On his way over to her house, he texted her and said he would be a few minutes late. She knew that he was bringing some gifts and replied to his text saying she wouldn't be there as she had left town.

My friend had driven two hours to go see her and they both had planned to meet at her house. Only at the last minute, 10 minutes before his arrival did she tell him that she wouldn't even be there. My friend replied to her text telling her that he could meet her somewhere else or drop the gifts off at her house. This was the absolute worst thing that he could have done.

The proper response would have been to tell her, "I will meet you at the house in 15 minutes as planned." She would either have said, "I am already out of town and can't make it," or she would have started to realize that she couldn't just disappear on him and she would have to show up to retrieve the gifts. Instead her reply to him was "just drop off my gifts at the house thank you."

They had a plan and committed to see each other on a certain time and date. His efforts showed his commitment and sincerity as he was driving two hours to make the appointment. As we talked about in Chapter 15, "You Teach People How to Treat You", he had programmed her that his time was not valuable and also that he would compromise and accept her behavior no matter what the inconvenience to him. She knew that disappearing at the last minute wouldn't have any bad consequences for her. She knew that she could do this, still get her gifts, and he would still talk to her.

Whenever someone disappoints you, you can't reward them for their actions and behavior. It must be absolutely clear to them that there are repercussions for their behavior and that it is unacceptable to you. This conforms with our two pillars as we are being completely open and honest with them and the mutual benefit is that both of us will be much happier in our relationship when neither one is disappointing the other.

Disappointment is often abuse. There's rarely a time that we don't know that what we are about to say or do will disappoint the other person. People who manipulate others for their own benefit don't feel regret about disappointing others; rather, they see it as a sign of strength and power in the relationship. These people know that they're going to disappoint the other person and not only don't feel bad about it, it's part of their plan to induce those feelings. This is obviously not healthy for any relationship and both sides lose much enjoyment by this behavior.

The solution is to program the person to not disappoint you intentionally. A major part of this is not to compromise and try to make it easier for the other person when they intentionally disappoint you. There must be repercussions for their intended behavior. If you're not compromising and dealing with it, they'll start to be programmed for change. In most cases people who intentionally take advantage of others and disappoint them have never had to compromise or make a decision. They intentionally disappoint multiple people in their lives and every one of them compromise making the bad behavior acceptable.

People often confuse forgiveness with compromise. Forgiveness is something you give when a person realizes, acknowledges and admits what they have done and makes a point to never do it again. This is not the case with most people who continually disappoint others because they are used to getting away with it. They never have to make a decision about losing someone because people compromise and accept their behavior.

If you don't compromise, the person will ultimately have to make a decision whether to change their behavior and treat you with respect, or to no longer associate with you. You add value to their life and that's why they want to be around you; however, they don't respect you and they disappoint you. Most often when faced with a choice they'll accept the programming and alter their behavior to keep you. What you'll find is more often than not people can actually avoid disappointing you and will choose to do so when you program them to avoid it.

Is it always possible for someone to avoid disappointing you? No. You must learn to recognize those occasions when someone made every possible effort and still let you down. Use programming only in those moments when you know a person has let you down when they could have made the choice to do otherwise.

CHAPTER 38
Consistency

Consistency is absolutely essential in programming behavior. Any deviation from the intended programming will result in loss of effectiveness and the person will revert back to the old behavior. As we will discuss in Chapter 42, resistance is a direct response that will come from a lack of consistency on your part in the brain coding. Consistency is the equivalent of discipline in brain coding and programming. It's an absolute parameter that will define whether the programming takes effect or not. Inconsistency on your part will nullify almost all of the brain code that you have written for them.

With brute force brain hacking you can take a little bit of time to get full effect and behavior modification. However, inconsistency can undo weeks or months of work instantly. Behavioral programming is similar to an antibiotic. It takes a full, consistent dose to have full effect. If a full dose is not taken, and that ailment has not been cured, a resistance to it will be developed. The result is that the next time you attempt to use the brain coding their resistance will be higher and you'll have a harder time programming them.

SECTION 6: DIGITAL DOWNLOADING

This is a section like no other! Here you'll learn how to change behavior remotely, from anywhere in the world, via texting and any other digital media formats. You don't need to be face-to-face, or even talking by phone, to program and alter behavior.

CHAPTER 39
LOL

Common acronyms and abbreviations can be an off switch when using digital media. It's extremely common for people to use such things as LOL, LMAO, etc. when texting and emailing people. Although these can be used effectively, most of the time they're beneficial only in response to the other person's text. The majority of the time people use these it's a digital "off switch," used by people that are timid about the statement that they just made.

LOL at the end of a sentence is usually the equivalent of that goofy fake smile people give you when that statement would be made face-to-face. When speaking to the person face-to-face you can say what you mean and then your body language hits the off switch. LOL and other such abbreviations at the end of your text is the same thing in digital form. You digitally hit the off switch in their brain and make the prior sentence null and void. You tell them that whatever you just said is a joke and not to take it too seriously. For the purposes of Behavioral Programming you should avoid using these abbreviations and acronyms in your digital messaging because you do want the other person to know that you are serious about what you say.

Another reason to avoid using these acronyms is because it's the same as everyone else and is a standard cookie-cutter response. If you want people to treat you like everyone else, then behave the same way they do. What we're doing with behavioral programming is coding their brain that we are different than everyone else and that their behavior must reflect that.

CHAPTER 40
Texting

In addition to being organic, one more major separation between Behavioral Programming and all other influence systems is that it can work entirely without personal contact, meaning this can be done entirely by text or email. This is very unique in psychology as no other system can completely be delivered through digital media. The cell phone now acts as a wireless router connecting us to someone's brain. We can access their thoughts from anywhere and at anytime that it's needed.

We can remotely program others via modern technology quickly and efficiently, and often times with better effects than seeing them in person. This has given us a new delivery system, a "wireless" link to their brain for coding. Face-to-

face conversations are like cables. They work, but have their limits. With Behavioral Programming there are no limits. Behavioral Programming is extremely efficient through digital media. No other contact is needed at all. You can completely program a person through texting. In some instances it may be your best option.

Only one other system touches on programming through digital communication. It's the system used by pick-up artists, and it only works because 1. Women love to text. 2. Women have better imaginations than men. In other words, women will insert all the good, juicy details into their heads that they would like to see when they read a text. So a pick-up artist's strategy is to use few details and let the women fill in the rest. The problem with seduction techniques is that they only initiate a physical contact. They work only in the short term. It's based on deceit and only benefits one side, the seducer's side.

Texting can often be the most efficient way to deliver programming. Men's brains think and process things more analytically so it's very natural for them. Women's brains will process your words much more literally because much of their communication and interpretation is done by body language and tone of voice. Since these are not present in text messages, women will rely on the words and then put their own spin on the emotion behind it. This can work wonderfully for both sexes.

One of the keys to understanding and decoding people's text messages is to understand the concept of a baseline for their behavior. The baseline is what we consider the norm, that which is normal and typical for that person in the environment and conditions. You can always tell when something is wrong with your significant other, close friend, or family member because they are behaving differently and out of character. When face-to-face, people who know each other very well can easily identify when something is out of the ordinary by the person's behavior.

In the new digital world we can do that remotely via text. All you must do is pay attention to people's normal behavior and habits when texting and establish a baseline for them. Only by learning what their normal behavior is can you then spot a change in them. Just as you notice how a friend stands, the clothes they wear, and their facial expressions, so must you pay attention to the frequency, context, subject matter, spelling, and other characteristics of their text messages. By paying attention to the specifics of their digital personality you can easily spot when something is different. Just as you make a mental note, most likely subconsciously, when someone has done something, you can do the same thing when they send you a text message.

For example, when you ask someone a question in a text and later find out that they were lying to you, go back through your text messages and look for the change in the baseline. That is how you will find their "tell." The next time you spot that personality characteristic in their text message you'll recognize it.

You can do this for nearly every personality trait from lying to crying. All you have to do is pay attention to the baseline and take mental notes. Texting is even easier than face-to-face for recognizing these traits as you're not simply relying on the accuracy of your memory, but you can always go back to the actual text conversation and view it. This will become very helpful to you as you remember to do this when something seems wrong. Learning to recognize when the other person is angry, unbelieving, excited, or crying will help you to understand the true emotion behind what they just said without being able to see or hear them.

When someone is lying in a text their baseline can change to something more aggressive, often accusatory and angry as well. They will typically increase the time delay between texts and will text more emotionally. Learn to recognize the baseline for each person when they're irritated, happy, mad, sad, and all of their other emotions. By developing this heightened sense of awareness your conversations will be much more productive. As you pay attention to specifics in their behavior, you'll learn to recognize each individual's personal emotion and characteristic that is attached to their writing style. Just as you have learned to recognize their habits, facial expressions, and body language when seeing them in person, you'll also learn to understand the emotions in their text messages.

For example, when a person is texting, separating a statement into a separate sentence or a different line shows that it is deliberate and it has more meaning. It shows that it's not an afterthought or a run-on sentence. When you hit the enter button and start a new sentence it's obvious to the reader that there is a gap and that it's a new sentence; hence, it is a separate point as well.

This can make a big difference in how a person's brain interprets the sentence and especially the emphasis and importance that they will subconsciously place on your statement. Separating different thoughts to a new line will clarify the point that you're making and will help the receiver of the message organize and understand your intentions. Because you've separated the ideas, they are now registered in their brain as separate thoughts causing less confusion, giving them the ability to easily process and contemplate your individual thoughts.

If multiple thoughts are crammed into the same sentence, typically only one idea alone will take dominance and will be considered for processing by the receiver's brain. The other contents of the sentence will most likely be ignored or receive very little attention. Typically, when you ask multiple questions in one sentence you'll get one answer as a reply. However by separating your questions or statements on different lines, the recipient understands that each individual statement or question is expected to be addressed.

Watch people's replies very carefully. One word replies are unacceptable, unless they're confirming that they received your data. What you can't accept are the useless one word answers that people will naturally give you if you let them. These replies are an insult. It means they just gave you the fastest, cookie-cutter response that they could punch into their phone. It tells you that they're not engaged in the conversation. It often times means that they could disagree, but don't care enough to type out a proper rebuttal and challenge your statement.

Whatever their motivation for giving you a one word reply, it's not good. Confusion is often not the case, but can be. More often a one-word answer is given for unbelief, disagreement, they're too busy for you, or they just don't care. The exception is when you've just delivered data to them via text, and they are acknowledging receipt, as in the following:

"I'll be there in 5."

"Ok."

The ok in this case is a good sign. Many people will leave you hanging when you text them information that requires no response. Those who do respond, even if it's only one word, are showing respect. This is really the only time that a one word reply is not a sign of something bad.

If you get one word replies from someone often, then you need to change that. You can do this by asking them to "explain" whenever they give you a single word answer. Either encourage them to engage you further, or tell them you can't talk right now. Another great way to get them to reply more appropriately is to ignore their text if it's only one word. If they really want to talk to you about it, then they'll text you again with a proper sentence.

While texting and communicating digitally use the same rewards and corrections to that you would use in person to modify behavior. Just as you do in face-to-face interactions you must understand how to effectively implement these techniques. Behavior can be modified with positive reinforcement of their actions that you approve of and also with a correction system for those actions that you do not approve of. As with everything else you must learn to identify the exact problems and issues to address and then respond with the appropriate programming to modify that behavior to something more acceptable.

One way to reward or correct behavior via text is by using a time delay. If the person you're communicating with is saying things that you don't approve of, a corrective action for this is to delay your response to their text. Whether they made a statement or asked an inappropriate question, this is for them. This is a form of correction and they will definitely notice that you're not excited to react to their last text.

When people make derogatory statements or ask sarcastic questions their intention is to engage in a verbal battle. What they're wanting is for you to engage them in a battle of wits and this action will only fuel their desire to continue, and most likely embolden them. By delaying your response you produce a dual benefit. A simple delay in time will start to cool them down and make them less passionate and eager to fight about the subject. It will also let them know that you won't respond to such treatment.

This is a double shot of programming, and the longer you delay the more effect it has on them. The corrective action of delaying your response to them will be interpreted in their brain as a punishment. They will notice that when they text you unpleasantries you will put them in "time out" and not talk to them.

The other side of the coin with this is the reward system for approved behavior. The amount of time delay can also be used as a reward to reinforce positive behavior that you approve of. Whenever possible, every time they do something that you approve of you can respond quickly and give them the attention that they're seeking. You can use timing in your responses to either correct or reinforce behavior.

Another effective way to reinforce approved behavior via texting is by saying thank you. Most people do not say this very often, especially in texts. You'll see all kinds of abbreviations, but rarely "thank you" all spelled out. Nothing registers in the subconscious the same as "thank you." Everything else registers as less than full appreciation. By texting "thank you," you will give positive reinforcement to correct behavior and encourage them to continue treating you in the same manner every time you correspond. "TY," "TM," "thx," and "thanx," all show some level of gratitude and can be used. Most people don't even use those enough to give the positive reinforcement needed to program people to maintain their current course of action.

Any appreciation will get results, but "thank you" will get the best results. Most people do not use the full thank you because they feel it's awkward and too formal to be used with friends. However, this is just not the case. The person receiving the thank you will never look at it weird, they will always get a good feeling every time they see it.

Along this same line we use another form of reward, and that's telling the person that you're happy. However you say it, letting the person know that what they just typed made you happy is an effective way to reward them and reinforce the behavior pattern. One word replies rarely accomplish this. Typically you will see things such as [Symbol] :) -_- "funny" "haha" and other responses that do not fully convey your appreciation for what they just typed. These are so standard that most people view them as filler and irrelevant. A typed out short sentence such as "that was great, thank you" or something similar will drive home the point much more effectively, and will set in the programming for similar continued behavior from them. If you get a silly face or a one-word response, always delay your reply. This will communicate to them that you put thought and effort into what you are saying to them because they are worth it, and you demand the same from them.

After a time delay let them know that their response was not adequate by repeating your last text. Copy and paste it. This is a clear indication to them that they need to respond differently than they did before. When they do, you reward them with your continued respectful and pleasant conversation. If they respond again, with a silly face or one word comment, you have two choices. The first is to increase your time delay in responding to them, and/or respond with a comment notifying them that you expect more of a response from them. An example may be; "I thought you would be more excited," or, "That's all you have to say?" or, "I guess you don't care." Any of these will convey your dislike for the lack of effort in their response.

So how do you convey feelings, emotions, and excitement in digital form?

One way is by typing differently than you usually do. This will convey feelings. For example, if you normally don't use abbreviations, then to use them shows fast, emotional typing. This can even show desperation in the right circumstances.

You've seen this before. Think back to when you were arguing with someone via text. You typed as fast as you could, and this normally includes taking shortcuts to write even faster by using abbreviations. You're sending texts in a hurry to get your thoughts to their head as fast as possible. The other person was most likely doing the same thing back to you. So by altering the way you type, they will note something is different.

Timing and spelling also play into this. Many people text properly and use autocorrect to send messages without many misspelled words and complete sentences. All of this can be modified when needing to express emotion through a text. Any and all abnormal message alterations will increase the effect of your words and it will bring emotion into the text. Their brain will register this subconsciously and you'll get the message delivered with the emphasis that you intended it to have and the passion that you felt as you wrote it.

Punctuation also comes into play here. Some people punctuate in texts and some don't. Whatever it is that you normally do, do the opposite. This will register differently than the normal dialog that you have with them. It works both ways. Say you always punctuate and spell properly. Typing fast and inaccurately and using no punctuation will register to them with emphasis on your emotional meaning behind the words. You're obviously passionate about what you just said because you typed fast, erratically, and didn't punctuate the sentence. On the other hand, if you normally do not use punctuation, then using it will have a special notice. When you put two exclamation marks behind your sentence, they will say, "Wow, they're really serious about this." Or if you now use a question mark they'll know that it's not a rhetorical question, and that you're raising your eyebrows while saying it. Any deviation from your normal baseline method of typing will add emotion to your texting.

A quite typical mistake people make while texting is "stacking up" their texts messages to a single person. This really creates several problems. First, it looks as if you have no one else to talk to. Looking desperate is rarely beneficial. It really doesn't matter what the content of your texts is (unless it's data, i.e. directions, etc.), it looks as though you have nothing better to do. It normally will not register with the other person as important or generate any sense of expediency on their part. It will often have the opposite effect. They won't want to look at them or pay attention to them. It's annoying to most people.

The other problem with "stacking" texts is that the person will often, very quickly skim over the texts only and then read the last one. This means they won't respond to any of the prior texts and you literally wasted your time typing them out. If you want a response to your earlier texts you will most likely have to send them again. The exception to this is when the person doesn't want to talk about the last text subject, and they'll pick one to reply to that they want to talk about. Make a mental note if this happens. This could also be done intentionally on your part to test a thought on someone. To see if they have any real interest in what you are saying (at least enough to take the time to write a reply) you can stack a few messages and see which ones they like. You may offer several options as questions, and the one that they talk about is the one they feel most strongly about.

The third problem with "stacking" texts is that you take away all the emphasis on what you previously wrote. By not getting a response and moving on yourself, you just reinforced their notion that your text isn't worth their time to respond to. This goes hand in hand with the fourth reason not to "stack." It trains the other person to behave with a lack of respect for you. Sometimes people are busy, we know this. You can't always answer texts as they come in. We know this. But by "stacking" them you show approval and acceptance of them ignoring you.

Remember, programming is what you're doing to people to establish a fully matured and healthy relationship. After that, most of these things don't apply to a real and close friend as we discussed earlier. These are all programming techniques to get others to conform to a healthy relationship.

If you can see a read receipt, don't send a new text until they read your last one. Read receipts are a great tool when texting. Watch how long it takes them to reply, and how long they blow you off. A long time frame displays a lack of respect, or a complete disinterest in what you're saying. This is obviously not the case with real and healthy friends, but a pretty good assumption with those who are in the programming phase of a relationship. Of course, it could also mean that they are legitimately busy, but if they are, and they really cared about you and the subject matter, they would text you back and say so. They would not wait for an hour after reading your text and then respond with one word or :).

Understand the baseline and watch when your conversation takes a different turn. Think about what you do when you are busy talking to someone and then your friend hits you up. You already have a conversation going and you don't want to be rude, so you respond to your friend but it's with much shorter replies and much longer time gap in between than normal. Very seldom will someone tell a good friend, or a superior, that they don't have time to talk. Most likely they'll attempt to pacify you by texting short, choppy, and sporadic replies to your text messages.

This is often something to consider when someone does tell you that they don't have time to talk. In most cases with people that you really care about offending, you won't tell them that you're too busy to talk. You'll simply try to make your best effort to hold a conversation with them. So when someone tells you that they're too busy to talk, for whatever reason, you can normally translate that into the fact that they have zero desire to talk to you right now. Most of the time it's because they don't want to talk, not because they actually can't.

If you really want to make a point with a text message, make it its own text. Don't write anything else in that text. Send it alone. One thing people often do is send a lot of information in one text and then hit send. The other person will not go line by line and start remarking to every line of your text. They will pick out what they feel is most important and comfortable to answer and respond to that.

Many people often browse over a larger text. This means that the person will most likely not take special notice of the item that you really want them to respond to. They'll choose to reply to whatever they want to address. Most likely they won't notice or give any special attention to the one point in particular that you were trying to make.

So if you're trying to make a point, make it its own text, hit send, and don't send another text until they have replied to that one. That way you'll know for sure that they've seen and read it, and it will be noticed and addressed properly.

Another mistake most people make is to confuse the recipient by running different subjects together. The easiest way to make your point is to start a new line for a new point. A new sentence on a new line puts emphasis on the statement before. It means that the first statement is not fluff or an intro to the next sentence, and that it is actually substantial on its own. If you run it all together, it becomes one paragraph, and hence people's minds go with the standard of one thought or subject per paragraph. People's texts often look like run on sentences or one big long paragraph. It's confusing to many, and it's also a great opportunity for the other person not to address an issue or question because it's mixed in with a "soup" of words.

Along this same line, when making a point, always delay the next text, or it will distract from the first. If you send separate texts rapidly, they will be recognized as one broken paragraph. Points of emphasis will lose meaning, and all of your texts will not be replied to. In fact, some of them will probably not even get read at all. So if you want to make a point with emphasis, then send it alone and wait to send the next text, even if a reply is not expected.

Separating a statement by a separate sentence or a different line shows that it is deliberate and it has more meaning. It shows them it is not an afterthought in a run-on sentence. Often people run things together in a text for expediency, and that is how people read it as well. If you don't take the time to make it stick out, then it probably won't to them either. They will most likely view it as an afterthought and not as the point of the whole text. So to make things clear, separate the different points with different texts sent and with time.

Sometimes in your life you will encounter those people that you never hear from until they want something. When you receive a request for something from such a person, simply reply after a delay, with a very short response. Never explain why you can't do it now. You most likely will start to ignore their calls and texts after you have figured this out. An easy way to start programming them is to delay your reply, suggesting to their subconscious that you are busy and that their request is not a priority to you, and then tell them you can't help them. On a separate line in a follow-up and separate text, invite them to join you in person for a get-together. Tell them you're busy now and can't help them tonight, but would like to see them for lunch tomorrow or any such thing.

This will send the signal that you can't be called out of the blue just to do favors for them. It will start to register with them that they need to be participating in your life if they want to gain the reward of your time and resources.

This also goes along with our next subject which is the person who ends a conversation. When texting with a person whom you are programming you always want to make sure that you're the person to end the conversation. This will develop a respect for your time, and put you in the Alpha position. They are most likely the one who texted you first, and then they decide when to end it. Break this habit and end the conversation first. This doesn't mean to break it off prematurely, or disrespect them by cutting them off, but you need to end the conversation while it's going well and things are good.

Remember, all of this is done while you are in the process of programming someone. These are not hard and fast rules for the people in your life that you already have a great relationship with. This is for those that need programming so that you can both benefit from a better relationship. Every so often a close friend goes a little off the range and must be programmed quickly to get things back to normal. These techniques can be used in those situations as well. Any time that you're not happy with your relationship with another person, all of these programming techniques can be used to get your relationship back on track.

You'll have some people in your life that will never require any thought or programming because your relationship has always been great. But for those other people in your life that need some social coaching, use these techniques to get everyone on the same page and feeling good again.

SECTION 7: SUCCESS AND TROUBLESHOOTING

In this section you'll learn how to tell if your programming has set in successfully and completely, and how to evaluate and make changes to your code if it didn't. Follow these simple guidelines to make it all work.

CHAPTER 41
Identifying Success

To be successful in your programming, there must be a way for you to gauge the effectiveness of your tactics. You must know when to turn up or down your tempo, and also when you need to move on to the next step. There are several indicators that you can use to determine if the person's response is in line with your programming or if they're still resisting and testing your commitment to this change.

When you challenge someone, there can be several levels of response from them. These range from completely unacceptable responses to several levels of acceptable response which help you gauge your progress.

The first level of response is unacceptable; it is ignoring, defiance, and aggressive or confrontational responses. An example of this may be a time when you ask your boyfriend a question and he answers with a smart remark. Or, he may just ignore your question or request altogether. He may even make a rude comment in reply. All of these are unacceptable responses. None of these are congruent with a healthy relationship. Therefore, these responses cannot be tolerated as that will only reinforce the behavior and make your relationship strained.

The levels of acceptable responses start with the lowest form of compliance. This is often mistaken by people as defiance, but in fact is evidence that the programming is taking effect and you are making progress with them. The first level of compliance is an excuse. When the person replies with an excuse, you need to recognize this as an act of compliance and progress on your part. This is a good thing.

Let's take that same example we just looked at. A girl asks her boyfriend if

157

he will make their date on time. The boyfriend replies, "No, I'm running late because of traffic." Whatever the excuse is, view this as the first stage of compliance to your programming. The fact that they feel the need to give you an excuse means that you are in the position of power and respect. A boss never makes excuses to his employees because the employees have no power over him, there are no repercussions, therefore no excuse is given or needed. Excuses are a sign of submission, and submission usually comes out of respect.

Think about it; you explain to your best friend the reason that you can't make it to his party because you respect him and don't want him to feel bad. It is out of respect for them that you give them an excuse so they don't think you intended to disappoint (disrespect) them. Submission is a sign of respect, and that is a good thing that should go both ways.

Most people would get upset and view an excuse as defiance or disrespect. The action may have been disrespectful, they may have been late showing up, but the excuse that they gave is a sign of submission, that they don't want to disappoint you. Your reply needs to acknowledge the submission and at the same time address the inappropriate behavior with a statement of non-satisfaction.

This may sound harsh, but it isn't. You will praise their submission statement and then gently let them know that you are disappointed in the action and would not like it repeated. An example may be like this: Your friend texts you and says he can't make it on time. You reiterate to him that he needed to be prompt for this function. He tells you that traffic is bad. You tell him a traffic jam is not his fault, but that he should have accounted for such things in his planning. That rewards him for his submissive and non-aggressive response, and at the same time suggests that you are still not satisfied with the action and you do not accept the excuse.

This response from you is non-aggressive because it doesn't challenge their honesty about their excuse. You believe the excuse, you just don't accept it as legitimate. Once you accept an excuse, it will be used over and over on you because you have endorsed it. You are the only person who teaches someone how to treat you. You are the only person who can endorse another person's behavior towards you. To have a healthy and lasting relationship, you must correct behavior that strains your relationship.

The second level of programming success is apology. When the person has enough respect for you they will apologize for their behavior that disappointed or disrespected you. This is always a good thing. It's an indication that they have developed a respect for you and desire you to respect them. Always recognize their apology and explain that with you things would have been different. An example of this could be: You ask your friend if they'll make it to a dinner party. They reply, "No, I'm sorry, I can't." You then tell them, "I see, I was hoping to introduce you to so and so, but maybe another time." "I see," acknowledges their apology without endorsing or showing approval, and the rest explains why they're losing out by not showing up. This is a polite and direct way to program them without offending and being rude. This will program them with a feeling of being left out, and they also had to submit and apologize for their action.

The next stage of programming success is apology plus excuse. This is about the most submissive that they can get and still have incorrect behavior. Their reply with this might be, "I'm sorry I can't make it to dinner. My car is acting up." This is usually the final stage of defiance and misbehavior before things really turn around. After this, with continued programming as laid out in this book, they'll be in full, healthy submissive behavior soon.

One thing to keep in mind is that someone you are programming may skip a step. It depends on where they were when you started programming them as to where they will be in this success gauge. They may go directly to step three and start there. They may stay a while at stage one. But this is a way for you to gauge behavioral modification. As we have stated before, these are only tools to be used on those whose behavior needs to changed. It is not for mature and healthy relationships. Although, if you have a great relationship and it starts to slip downward, these can all be applied to get things back to where they should be.

CHAPTER 42
Resistance

When you first start to program someone you may experience signs of resistance from them. This is completely normal and it doesn't mean that the programming isn't working. The programming is working but the resistance you're sensing from them is signs of shock to their system and often times a test as well. It is a shock to their system because you've suddenly, and abruptly, slightly changed your communication with that person. Although they can't pinpoint it exactly most of the time, they will sense that something is different and may resist or appear to be resisting the programming.

The other part of this is that they're testing you. Because they've gotten away with their behavior throughout your entire relationship they'll most certainly test you to see if you're serious or if they'll be allowed to continue the current behavior. Often it may be better to use a form of digital communication when you first begin your programming and coding of their brain. This is because most of the time people don't have the confidence that they need when they're delivering the programming to the other person. Often as people first attempt brain coding they're timid and they'll hit the off switch, completely shutting down the programming operation.

Using digital media for your first brain coding exercises can be a good idea. The coding will work and the programming will set in, provided you don't add modifiers that hit the off switch. These are most easily avoided in the beginning by using text or email to start the programming. The tone of your voice, your facial expressions, and other body language can hit the off switch, which is all avoided using digital media. This is all discussed in the chapter on digital media.

As you get further along in your programming and your brute force brain hacking is in full effect, you'll experience less and less resistance. They may occasionally offer slight resistance but at that point it's simply a small test to see if they can program you to go back to the way it was or if this is the new standard. As we discussed before, consistency is the key and you must be dedicated to your programming endeavors.

CHAPTER 43
Challenges

How do you to respond to challenges? An aggressive defense gives the other person's questions credibility. An immediate and deliberate dismissal, such as using the word "anyway" and then ignoring the challenge and moving on can be effective. If it's a legitimate question then it should be handled appropriately. If it is a question challenging you, or a remark of denial, then seldom does arguing change their opinion.

There will always be challenges due to people's positions regarding an Alpha status. The higher you climb towards being the top Alpha, the less challenges you will get. When someone challenges you that means they do not accept you as the Alpha. Most likely they recognize that the others hold you as the Alpha and this is their attempt to raise their status above yours.

Many people will argue just to argue. The fact that you use your time and energy to argue with them raises their status because you recognize their position. Your arguing means the other person has a legitimate point, and the acknowledges the possibility that you are wrong. Healthy intellectual conversations are a good thing; however, challenges don't fit in this category. Unless it's mandatory that you argue and prove your point, the best answer is normally not to argue with that person.

From the onset of a challenge from another person, that person's purpose is to prove some kind of point. They may want to prove you wrong altogether, or they want to show that they're your intellectual equal, or they may be trying to simply show that they have something of value to add to the conversation. The problem with all of these motives is that they never started the argument to get to the truth.

They started it to distract from it. So by arguing in return you are just adding fuel to their fire.

You can rarely win an argument, they usually just end up with two or more upset people. The other person doesn't want to see what your position is, they simply must argue a point to raise their status. Knowing this up front, we know that we can't get into an argument with people.

If the other person is arguing, they are not going to change their mind no matter what is said. If a person is inquisitive and asking an honest question, then you have a conversation, not an argument. The odds of you winning an argument, the other person ending up agreeing with you, not offending other people who may be listening, and coming out with more points than you started with is astronomically low. It's not going to happen. So stay out of arguments and avoid the big negatives that go with it.

CHAPTER 44
Social Influence

You must be careful about how you make your suggestions look and sound around other people. The group's perception of your words and intentions can prove critical to success in some situations. If it sounds bad to others, they'll advise your subject not to comply. You must appeal to the entire crowd when others are present.

People have experienced this many times. The following story illustrates this: A guy meets a girl at a club. He is about to leave with her, and her girlfriend steps in and squashes it. At this point the others around them have more influence than you do over them. If you haven't made them comfortable, their friends will dissuade them from compliance. If you aren't liked and trusted by their friends, you'll most likely not win over your subject.

I'm not implying that you must be deceitful with the crowd, I'm saying that you can't ignore the crowd and focus solely on your subject. At this point they must all be your focus until you can separate your target from the group.

There are several ways to "win the crowd." The first is to be yourself and fit into the group and contribute. This means be an interesting and participating member of the group. Interact with them as though they're your friends too. Another way is to pay attention to the conversation and tone of the conversation of the group, and find a way to agree with them and contribute to their point of view. This will definitely help to win over the crowd, and gain needed rapport.

During all of this you don't need to lie about who you are or what you stand for, you simply find a way to agree with them on some detail of what they are saying. You don't have to compromise your beliefs to have a pleasant and engaging conversation with someone who believes differently than you. That being said, you must always remember not to argue. Arguing will shut down passive programming immediately. You simply listen to what they're saying, and find something in common to agree upon and discuss.

By engaging the group, and taking part in their conversations you will be accepted into the group and people will "approve" of you. This is a critical part of getting to someone in a crowd. You must not scare their "pack." They must be accepting of you because at this point you have no influence over your target subject. Your target subject has a good relationship with their pack and will be influenced by them, to either accept you or not accept you.

One way to get the attention of the target subject in a crowd is by using the "hard to get" principle. People want things that are hard to get. The way to apply this in a crowd situation is to not give the target subject all of your attention. Don't ignore them completely, just engage the others in the group more frequently, and with more intent.

This will make you "hard to get" for your target subject, and will also keep the group happy as you are engaging nicely with them. So when you do move on to your intended subject, the group will be fine with that, and by this time the subject is dying to engage you more fully. This is not being sneaky, this is just presenting yourself in a more valuable way. You're not being fake or deceitful, you're simply using their default brain programming to gain approval and interest.

It's just a matter of understanding brain code and how it works. You want to make a new friend. You want the attention and interaction with a specific person in a group. Knowing how the brain works allows you to effectively interact with everyone and get the outcome that you desire. Your goal is to start a relationship with someone new. You do have something to offer that person, and you do have good intentions. This is a system that uses natural, default human brain coding to get the results that you want in a given situation.

Everyone has their own "pack," and we all listen to their advice on given subjects and people. You must know how to gain acceptance and rapport with the entire group to be able to effectively select one out of the group to befriend. While they're with their pack, you must build rapport and acceptance from the majority of the pack. This is true most of the time even after you have them alone. To keep a relationship with that person, you'll need to continue to keep your acceptance with the group until you have more influence over that person than their group does.

CHAPTER 45
Anchors

People often find themselves in relationships with someone who has recently or maybe not so recently gotten out of a relationship, and they can't seem to get a real and strong connection with them. It seems as though the other person is still holding on to that last person that they were with. What is baffling is that they ended the relationship because it was not happy and healthy, and yet their mind is constantly thinking about that other person and they can't let them go.

This is very frustrating to the new person in a relationship and is often the cause of many relationships being ended before they even mature. The reason for this is what we call emotional anchoring. Because your relationship with this person is new you don't have as many experiences or the opportunity for them to emotionally attach or anchor themselves to you yet.

Everyone needs to be grounded and have a solid base to work from. It's like an emotional savings account. So the relationship with the other person may have ended officially, and it was overall not very happy, but it's still a place that they could go back to if they had to. The other person is an emotional reserve in case everything else falls through.

Just as people will panic when their savings and reserve funds are completely diminished, so will people collapse emotionally if they don't have their anchor. It doesn't matter how strong, how big, or how bad the anchor is, when everything falls apart they know they can always go back to that and count on that. It may not be great, but at least it's something.

People will hold on to and come back to the last best emotional attachment they had, which right now is the most recent one they left. They'll continue to do so until you replace them and become that emotional anchor. It depends on the emotional and mental status of the person as to how long it will take to make you that emotional anchor. With some people it can take one incident of you showing your true intentions to become that person, with others it can take a while. With Behavioral Programming you will treat people in a way that will make them happy, so it doesn't take long to become the new emotional anchor and prove you're adding value to their lives.

People get frustrated in new relationships when the other person won't abandon their last significant other. They often times will continue dialog with them and even continue to see them in person. Know that that person is currently their emotional anchor, but that through the programming you will become that emotional anchor for them. They'll be able to completely detach from the other person as your relationship matures. Don't get jealous or angry that they hold on to the last one they had for a while. Once they are convinced that you are genuine and adding value to their life, they'll anchor to you and leave the other person in the past.

CHAPTER 46
Relapse

Most people are not 100% satisfied with the way they are treated by other people; however, they are quite comfortable with their treatment of others. This is a very important distinction to remember, as it can have a tremendous impact on the success of your programming. They may not particularly like how they treat you but they are satisfied with the overall effect.

This can be thought of as similar to a drug addiction. The person's treatment of you is as addictive as illicit drugs. Once you start your programming on that person, you have now altered the norm and they will feel the effects. They will most likely start to resist. This concept works hand-in-hand with consistency. As you start your programming on the person they will most likely want to reject it because you are altering their drug, i.e. their treatment of you, from the way it has always been. Their addiction to this behavior has become normal and is quite strong and they won't want to change. They are comfortable with the way it is right now.

As we have discussed, it is absolutely essential to be consistent. What we must avoid is allowing a relapse. The same as addiction to a drug, anytime the person relapses and takes another hit, or in this case, goes back to treating you the same, most of the hard work in changing their behavior is gone. Also, like any addiction, many times their relapse will put them back to square one and the time starts all over again for recovery and change. Resistance is normal and expected, but resistance will turn to relapse when their challenge (reverting back to their old behavior with you) is not properly and immediately addressed by you.

When a person reverts back to their usual behavior with you, you must continue the programming and remain consistent. You can't let it go unchallenged even once. A single resistance to your programming that's perceived as accepted by you will cause a relapse. They will subconsciously receive that as you caving in and they will immediately go back to their old behavior and treatment of you.

Most of the resistance on their part will be at a conscious level. Especially in the beginning they will be testing you to see if this is really the new way things are going to be. After a relapse things become more subconscious to them and they will not actively think about their behavior. They will simply revert back to habits and past performance and the results will dictate their actions.

You must avoid at all costs letting them relapse. You completely control whether their behavior is resistance or progresses into relapse. It's all controlled by how you react to their attempts to resist the change. When an attempt is made on their part to challenge or resist the new standard you have set forth in your programming you must deal with it sternly and consistently. You must react the same way that you reacted when you first started programming them.

SUMMARY

Most people are not 100% satisfied with the way they are treated by other people; however, they are quite comfortable with their treatment of others. This is a very important distinction to remember, as it can have a tremendous impact on the success of your programming. They may not particularly like how they treat you but they are satisfied with the overall effect.

This can be thought of as similar to a drug addiction. The person's treatment of you is as addictive as illicit drugs. Once you start your programming on that person, you have now altered the norm and they will feel the effects. They will most likely start to resist. This concept works hand-in-hand with consistency. As you start your programming on the person they will most likely want to reject it because you are altering their drug, i.e. their treatment of you, from the way it has always been. Their addiction to this behavior has become normal and is quite strong and they won't want to change. They are comfortable with the way it is right now.

As we have discussed, it is absolutely essential to be consistent. What we must avoid is allowing a relapse. The same as addiction to a drug, anytime the person relapses and takes another hit, or in this case, goes back to treating you the same, most of the hard work in changing their behavior is gone. Also, like any addiction, many times their relapse will put them back to square one and the time starts all over again for recovery and change. Resistance is normal and expected, but resistance will turn to relapse when their challenge (reverting back to their old behavior with you) is not properly and immediately addressed by you.

When a person reverts back to their usual behavior with you, you must continue the programming and remain consistent. You can't let it go unchallenged even once. A single resistance to your programming that's perceived as accepted by you will cause a relapse. They will subconsciously receive that as you caving in and they will immediately go back to their old behavior and treatment of you.

Most of the resistance on their part will be at a conscious level. Especially in the beginning they will be testing you to see if this is really the new way things are going to be. After a relapse things become more subconscious to them and they will not actively think about their behavior. They will simply revert back to habits and past performance and the results will dictate their actions.

You must avoid at all costs letting them relapse. You completely control whether their behavior is resistance or progresses into relapse. It's all controlled by how you react to their attempts to resist the change. When an attempt is made on their part to challenge or resist the new standard you have set forth in your programming you must deal with it sternly and consistently. You must react the same way that you reacted when you first started programming them.

AFTERWORD

"To track is to live the life of the quarry; mentally, spiritually, and physically. Very few trackers ever reach this level of mastery because they are unwilling to leave the "self" behind in order to become that which they seek...behaviorally. Instead, they track themselves, their fears, desires, preconceptions, and inventions which they overlay on their human quarry.

Through focused inspection of the essence of the two pillars of honesty and mutual benefit contained in this book on Behavioral Programming, Mr. Alwood will help you index your human interactive skills against salient truths that have always existed with those few, like Mr. Alwood, who have shadowed all living things to read the human behaviors of the human-to-human communication pattern. Mr. Alwood's method of behavioral programming is lost to those who are asphyxiated on the technological footprint call industrial efficiency. But, is this true efficiency or the degradation and desensitizing of our true nature?

Behavioral Programming is the "heart" of the matter. A "window" through which reveals the beautiful and foundational knowledge provided by a lifetime of tutelage at the feet of an astute observer of human nature. To Mr. Alwood, my brother, I say well done. You have brought us all back to where every trail begins and ends; the "Behavior" of the human being as programmed through interactive communication verbally as well as non-verbally. Through your book, we can all now command how our relationships will turn out through your precedent   setting Behavioral Programming.

Cmdr. Ty Cunningham, MMAS, CMST

Owner, Chief Tracker, and Lead Instructor

Supervisory Deputy U.S. Marshal (Ret) and Fmr. Commander of the Alaska U.S. Marshals Tactical Tracking Unit (TTU)

Made in the USA
Middletown, DE
20 June 2023

33047024R00106